OPTICAL CHARACTER RECOGNITION:

An Illustrated Guide to the Frontier

THE KLUWER INTERNATIONAL SERIES
IN ENGINEERING AND COMPUTER SCIENCE

OPTICAL CHARACTER RECOGNITION:

An Illustrated Guide to the Frontier

by

Stephen V. Rice
Comparisonics Corporation

George Nagy
Rensselaer Polytechnic Institute

Thomas A. Nartker
University of Nevada, Las Vegas

KLUWER ACADEMIC PUBLISHERS
Boston / Dordrecht / London

Distributors for North, Central and South America:
Kluwer Academic Publishers
101 Philip Drive
Assinippi Park
Norwell, Massachusetts 02061 USA
Telephone (781) 871-6600
Fax (781) 871-6528
E-Mail <kluwer@wkap.com>

Distributors for all other countries:
Kluwer Academic Publishers Group
Distribution Centre
Post Office Box 322
3300 AH Dordrecht, THE NETHERLANDS
Telephone 31 78 6392 392
Fax 31 78 6546 474
E-Mail <orderdept@wkap.nl>

Electronic Services <http://www.wkap.nl>

Library of Congress Cataloging-in-Publication Data

Rice, Stephen V.
Optical character recognition : an illustrated guide to the frontier / by Stephen V. Rice, George Nagy, Thomas A. Nartker.
p. cm. -- (Kluwer international series in engineering and computer science : SECS 502)
Includes bibliographical references and index.
ISBN 0-7923-8492-X (alk. paper)
1. Optical character recognition devices. I. Nagy, George. II. Nartker, Thomas A. III. Title. IV. Series.
TA1640.R53 1999
006.4'24--dc21 99-20879
CIP

Printed on acid-free paper.

Printed in the United States of America

Contents

Preface

We are fortunate to have participated in a multi-year effort at the University of Nevada, Las Vegas, to evaluate OCR systems that recognize machine-printed characters on document pages. A test of leading systems was conducted each year from 1992 through 1996. These tests have provided OCR users, researchers, and product developers with a clearer understanding of the state of the art. Each of our test reports displays characters that were difficult for participating systems to recognize. These pictures of problems have been so popular that we decided to create an entire book of them, organized by problem category.

OCR systems often make errors that are surprising or non-intuitive. For users of these systems, this book explains which document characteristics are troublesome and why. For OCR researchers looking for problems to solve at the leading edge, and for OCR developers seeking to improve their products, this book illuminates the frontier. Our sincerest hope is that it will inspire great achievements in the field.

We are indebted to the many people who have influenced this book: Carl Alsing, Andrew Bagdanov, Henry Baird, Mindy Bokser, Roger Bradford, Phil Cheatle, Elaine Hayden, Tin Kam Ho, Jonathan Hull, Frank Jenkins, Junichi Kanai, Daniel Lopresti, Prateek Sarkar, Barbara Cerny Shirley, Elisa Barney Smith, Ben Wittner, and Yihong Xu. Thanks also to Dave Melton for the delightful artwork.

— Stephen V. Rice, George Nagy, and Thomas A. Nartker, 1999

Chapter 1

Introduction

"I am fluent in over six million forms of communication."

— the robot C-3PO in *Return of the Jedi*, 20th Century Fox, 1983

Science-fiction authors have long imagined robots with cognitive and linguistic abilities. Hollywood's portrayals of androids foretell a fascinating world of computer creations.

But where are we today? Will computer technology ever fulfill the predictions of futurists? This book considers one of the many problems in artificial intelligence: the identification of characters on a document page. The field is known as Optical Character Recognition or OCR. How far has technology advanced in this field?

A document page may contain characters printed by machine (like this page), printed by hand, or handwritten in cursive script. In this book, we focus on the easiest of these to recognize: machine-printed characters.

Systems for recognizing machine-printed text originated in the late 1950s and have been in widespread use on desktop computers since the early 1990s. Much of the world's information is held captive in hard-copy documents. OCR systems liberate this information by converting the text on paper into electronic form. Once in this form, information retrieval systems can be employed to locate material of interest, and word processing software can be utilized to edit the text.

However, OCR systems do not perform this conversion flawlessly. They make errors, and the electronic version of a document may not properly match the paper version. What if an OCR system cannot reliably distinguish the letter c from the letter e? You may cnd up with a scntcnec that looks likc this. Imagine an entire page of such gibberish. In such cases, it is more efficient to type the contents of the entire page into the computer than to correct the errors in the OCR output. *An OCR system that makes too many mistakes is not useful.*

OCR technology has advanced to the point where today's systems are indeed useful for processing a large variety of machine-printed documents. Accuracies of 99% or more are routinely achieved on cleanly-printed pages. But there is much room for improvement, and this book attempts to characterize the problems that need to be solved to advance the state of the art. Keep in mind that even 99% accuracy translates into 30 errors on a typical page containing 3,000 characters.

We utilized three leading OCR systems to process pages from four types of documents: technical reports, magazine articles, newspaper articles, and business letters. Using a scanner, each page was digitized at a resolution of 300 dots per inch to produce a bi-level image, which was submitted to each system for conversion. To locate errors, OCR output was compared with correct text using a string-matching algorithm.

We randomly selected about 1,000 words and phrases in which more than one system made an error and then analyzed these snippets to determine the likely sources of error. We organized these sources into a taxonomy that provides the structure of this book. In Chapter 2, we present recognition problems caused by imaging defects, specifically heavy print, light print, stray marks, and curved baselines. Chapter 3 is devoted to cleanly-printed, but similar-looking symbols. Punctuation characters deserve special treatment, which they receive in Chapter 4. Typographic features that confound OCR systems are described in Chapter 5. Lastly, in Chapter 6, we discuss some techniques for advancing the state of the art, and we mention other sources of error not covered in the previous chapters.

This book contains 280 examples that illustrate problems at the leading edge of OCR. Each example presents a small portion of a page image, first in its original size and then magnified by a factor of four to make it easier for humans to discern minute details of the characters. The correct text, which is the desired output from an OCR system, appears next, followed by the outputs from the three leading systems. We refer to these systems anonymously as Device 1, Device 2, and Device 3.

Correct text and OCR output are displayed throughout this book using the OCR-B typeface. This typeface, along with OCR-A, was designed to make it easier for OCR systems to distinguish similar symbols such as 1 (one), l (ell), I (eye), 0 (zero), and O (oh). We use it here to benefit human readers.

A tilde (~) in the OCR output is a *reject character* produced by a system to indicate that it is unable to recognize one or more characters in the image. OCR output is displayed as <nil> when a system has produced no output.

The examples are numbered consecutively within each section of the book. Thus, the second example in Section 5.5 is numbered *02*, and is referred to as *5.5-02*, or simply *02* when in Section 5.5.

Example *5.5-02* is shown below. A snippet of a page image is reproduced in its original size at the top center of the figure and is followed by its 4X magnification. The desired OCR output appears next (BRIDGE PARKWAY), followed by the outputs from the three OCR systems. Device 1 produced BPIDGE PARKWAY, erroneously generating a P for the R in BRIDGE; Device 2 was confused and produced no output at all, which is indicated by <nil>; and Device 3 generated a reject character for the B and an F for the E in BRIDGE.

5.5 *02*

BRIDGE PARKWAY

BPIDGE PARKWAY

<nil>

~RIDGF PARKWAY

The following table shows how the 280 examples are divided by section and document type. Information on the source of each example is provided in the Appendix.

Section	Number of Examples				Total
	Technical	Magazine	Newspaper	Letter	
2 Imaging Defects					
2.1 Heavy Print	23	7	4	1	35
2.2 Light Print	21	3	2	9	35
2.3 Heavy and Light Print	3	1	0	4	8
2.4 Stray Marks	5	2	8	2	17
2.5 Curved Baselines	6	0	0	0	6
3 Similar Symbols					
3.1 Similar Vertical Symbols	13	5	3	1	22
3.2 Other Similar Symbols	19	2	1	3	25
4 Punctuation					
4.1 Commas and Periods	10	5	5	5	25
4.2 Quotation Marks	8	3	0	1	12
4.3 Special Symbols	7	2	0	1	10
5 Typography					
5.1 Italics and Spacing	4	6	2	5	17
5.2 Underlining	7	0	0	1	8
5.3 Shaded Backgrounds	0	5	3	0	8
5.4 Reverse Video	0	8	3	2	13
5.5 Unusual Typefaces	2	4	1	2	9
5.6 Very Large Print	1	4	10	0	15
5.7 Very Small Print	4	4	1	6	15
Total	133	61	43	43	280

Some sources of error appeared more often in some document types than in others. Many of the technical reports were photocopies and were therefore more prone to imaging defects than the other document types, although stray marks occurred most often in the newspaper examples. Shaded backgrounds and reverse video were most common in the magazine articles. Many of the examples exhibit multiple sources of error and could fit into more than one section of the book.

The three OCR systems make different errors, but they are very close to one another in terms of overall accuracy. (This was observed not only on the 280 examples but also using much larger collections.) All three systems produced no errors on 13-16% of the examples, one error on 33-36% of the examples, and two or more errors on 51-52% of the examples. A test of the ability of children to identify the characters in these examples indicates that the computer systems lag far behind:

	No Errors	One Error	Multiple Errors
Device 1	16%	33%	51%
Device 2	13%	36%	51%
Device 3	15%	33%	52%
Child, age 7	58%	23%	19%
Child, age 10	86%	10%	4%
Child, age 14	92%	6%	2%

A lexicon containing thousands of words is a tool used by every leading OCR system to improve its accuracy. It is essential for resolving ambiguities. Suppose a system is unsure whether a word is cnd or end. By checking its lexicon, the system discovers that end is a valid word, but cnd is not. Only in the rare circumstance when cnd appears on the page will the system choose incorrectly. However, if both choices belong to the lexicon (e.g., cat and eat), or neither choice can be found (e.g., Madcra and Madera), the lexicon cannot help with the decision. Humans also possess a lexicon that assists them in recognition. It is interesting that despite his diminutive lexicon, the seven-year-old boy who took part in this test identified characters with far greater accuracy than the leading OCR systems.

It is surprising that after more than 40 years of research, OCR systems are not close to matching human performance. This book outlines areas in which today's systems can be improved. The examples illustrate the limitations of current systems, yet many times they showcase their impressive abilities. Although we provide the commentary, the examples tell the story.

Chapter 2

Imaging Defects

> A heap of broken images, where the sun beats,
> And the dead tree gives no shelter.
>
> — from *The Waste Land* by T. S. Eliot, 1922

Even if text is printed in a common, easy-to-recognize typeface and format, many errors are caused by imaging defects. These defects are introduced somewhere along the way between the printing process and the page image that is submitted to the OCR system. Such defects consist of heavy, smeared, touching characters (Section 2.1), light and broken characters (Section 2.2), or a combination of the two (Section 2.3). Stray marks (Section 2.4) and curved baselines (Section 2.5) are also troublesome.

Defects may arise as soon as the slug or printhead hits the paper. Porous paper causes the ink to spread or bleed through from the reverse side. Coated, glossy paper does not absorb ink or toner, but is liable to smudging. Very high-speed printers, like newspaper presses, typically produce fuzzier type. New, heavily-inked typewriter or printer ribbons can create blotchy characters, while worn ribbons produce faint impressions. Photocopying the page, especially on older copiers, results in further loss of definition. Copying the copies rapidly escalates the deterioration: even with modern technology, tenth-generation copies are barely legible.

The scanning process introduces imperfections of its own. The part of the page under the scanner head is illuminated by a fluorescent light. Each scanner detector collects light focused on, and reflected from, a minute area of the page. The light sensitivity of a sensor element about the center of this spot is called the *point-spread function* of the scanner, and the diameter of the area of high sensitivity is called the *spot diameter*. The larger the spot, the more the digital output is influenced by light originating closer to the centers of adjacent sensors. The amount of light collected during a brief interval (about one microsecond) is converted to an electrical signal. In bi-level scanning, where the page is converted to an array of 0's and 1's known as a bi-level image, these signals are thresholded. That is, a signal larger than the threshold value (lots of light reflected from the page) is converted to a 0 (white), while a small signal (little reflection) is converted to a 1 (black).

At high thresholds, a large point-spread function thickens the character because just outside the perimeter of the character, not enough light is reflected to trigger a 0. At low thresholds, a large point-spread function thins the image, because just inside the perimeter, there is enough light for a 0. With the same point-spread function, lowering the threshold always makes the characters thinner. The point-spread function is a property of the scanner optics and electronics, and cannot be changed by the operator. However, the scanning software usually permits the user to adjust the threshold through a "brightness control." The choice of threshold affects OCR accuracy because low thresholds give rise to fragmented characters, and high thresholds create touching characters. The threshold may also fluctuate because of electronic or thermal noise, and the sensitivity itself may vary among sensor elements because of imperfections of the manufacturing process. Hence, identical characters on different parts of the page may result in different bi-level images.

Paper is not a very high-contrast medium. The amount of light reflected from white bond paper is only about twenty times as much as that from solid, dark type printed on that paper. With high-contrast film, ratios of several hundred to one are achievable, which is why it is used as the master image in high-quality typesetters. The ratio of sunlight to starlight reflected by white sand in a desert is over a million to one. The sun is more than a billion times brighter than a distant star, yet the human eye can perceive both. Even the most sensitive gray-scale scanner does not offer anywhere near the dynamic range of the pupil-retina combination.

Therefore, scanners are much more vulnerable than human readers to low contrast and to variations in the foreground and background reflectance of the page.

Printing and scanning at finite resolution are sources of imperfection. Typically, a page is sampled horizontally and vertically at a rate of 300 dots per inch (dpi). All of the examples in this book were scanned at this resolution. A higher sampling rate can be used, such as 400 or 600 dpi, but it may be of little or no benefit to an OCR system tuned to 300 dpi. Most OCR systems accept a facsimile (fax) image of a page. This is a low-resolution bi-level image sampled horizontally at 204 dpi and vertically at either 98 dpi (standard mode) or 196 dpi (fine mode). Error rates are much higher on fax images.

Geometric distortions may be introduced at every stage (printing, copying, faxing or scanning) by imperfect optics and by ragged motion of the paper or sensor assembly.

In gray-level scanning, an integer value in the range 0 to 255 is generated to indicate the amount of reflected light, with the highest value corresponding to white. In a gray-scale image, one byte is needed for each pixel to store this value. The current trend in OCR is to accept as input a gray-scale image of a page, which allows a more detailed analysis of digital patterns, and has been shown to reduce the error rate on low-contrast material. It can be argued that gray-scale information effectively increases the resolution of the scanner, and therefore yields lower error rates on high-contrast text with small or closely-spaced characters. However, processing a gray-scale image requires more computation and substantially more storage than a bi-level image of the same page. Hence, computers with faster microprocessors, and more RAM and disk storage, are needed. As colored copy becomes more prevalent in the workplace due to the increased availability of color printers and copiers, we can expect color scanners to emerge as a tool to facilitate the recognition of colored documents.

2.1 Heavy Print

Character segmentation is the process of locating the individual characters within a word. When neighboring characters are joined or fused due to heavy print, an OCR system must perform the delicate task of separating them. Even for characters that are easily isolated, heavy print can distort their shapes, making them unidentifiable.

Capital letters tend to have similar, blocky shapes. With no ascenders or descenders to help distinguish them, they can be difficult to segment and identify. TEXT SET ENTIRELY IN CAPITALS IS ALSO MORE DIFFICULT FOR HUMANS TO READ. (SOME OF US REMEMBER STRUGGLING TO READ TEXT PRODUCED ON UPPERCASE-ONLY CHAIN PRINTERS.)

In *01*, the M looks like an N to Device 1, and an L to Device 2. The M's resemble H's in *02*. A few important pixels in the trough of the second M enable Device 3 to recognize it. None of the systems can identify the filled-in M of *03*.

2.1 *01*

Mission

Mission

Mission

Nission
Lission
Mission

2.1	*02*

Man-Made

Man-Made

Man-Made

Han-Hade
Man-Made
Han-Made

2.1	*03*

Unnamed Mineral

Unnamed Mineral

Unnamed Mineral

Unnamed H1nere1
Unnamed Nineral
Unnamed wineral

In *04*, the touching serifs cause two systems to mistake the H for a B, although the presence of Bolt, but not Holt, in the lexicon may have contributed. The systems find three different interpretations for the 9 in *05*, whose oversized bowl touches the bottom loop.

2.1 *04*

Holt (1984).

Holt (1984).

Holt (1984).

Bolt (1984).
Holt (1984).
Bolt (1984).

2.1 *05*

1984

1984

1984

1U84
IOS4
1Q84

An unexpected confusion arises in *06*, where back-to-back parentheses are interpreted as the letter X by two systems.

2.1 *06*

section 102(2XC)

section 102(2XC)

```
section 102(2)(C)

section 102(2XC)
section 102(2)(C)
section 102(2XC)
```

In all-uppercase words, portly M's may crowd adjacent letters, as in *07*, where the M and E are virtually unseparable. The example in *08* features Siamese M's that baffle all three systems. Note that small pieces are missing from the second M, the first N, and the D. Images that exhibit both heavy and light print are discussed in Section 2.3.

2.1 *07*

MECHANICAL

MECHANICAL
FECHANICAL
~CHANICAL

2.1 *08*

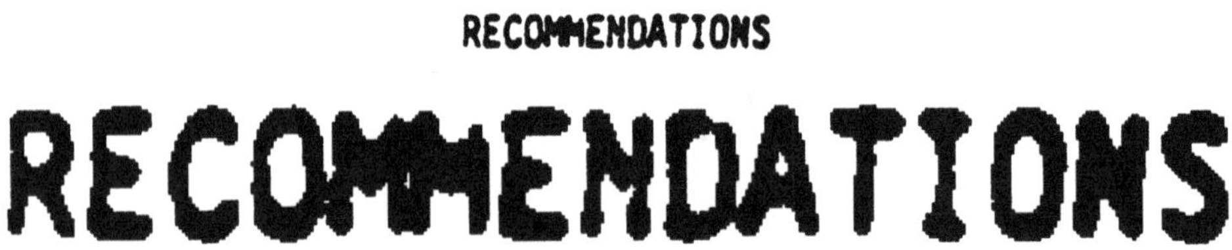

RECOMMENDATIONS

RECDmENDATIONS
RECO~HENDATIDNS
REC~ENDATIOffS

In *09*, only one of the systems interprets the closed S's correctly, and all have severe difficulty with the rest of the phrase. In *10*, seven consecutive characters are joined, and remarkably, one system can read it. Device 3 generated ANTS, a desperate grab from its lexicon.

2.1 *09*

See HISTORY,

See HISTORY,

See HISTORY,

Bee E18TORY,
See IiISTQRY,
8"HIBTORY,

2.1 *10*

CONTENTS

CONTENTS

CONTENTS

CONTENTS
CGIENTS
ANTS

In segmenting the first word of *11*, Device 1 evidently cuts off the first character too soon, converting the L to an I. The other systems exhibit a similar fault in *12*, converting the L to lowercase. In addition, the hyphen attached to the first p is overlooked.

2.1 *11*

LAS VEGAS,

LAS VEGAS,

LAS VEGAS,

INS VEGAS,
LAS VEGAS,
[AS VEGAS,

2.1 *12*

Lap-top

Lap-top

Lap-top

Lap-top
laptop
laptop

The *x-height* letters, a c e m n o r s u v w x z, have no ascenders or descenders and are especially prone to confusion due to heavy print. Filled-in s's are particularly troublesome, as shown in *13* and *14*.

2.1 *13*

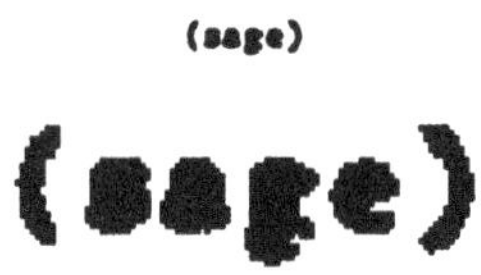

(sage)

(age)
(aage)
(sage)

2.1 *14*

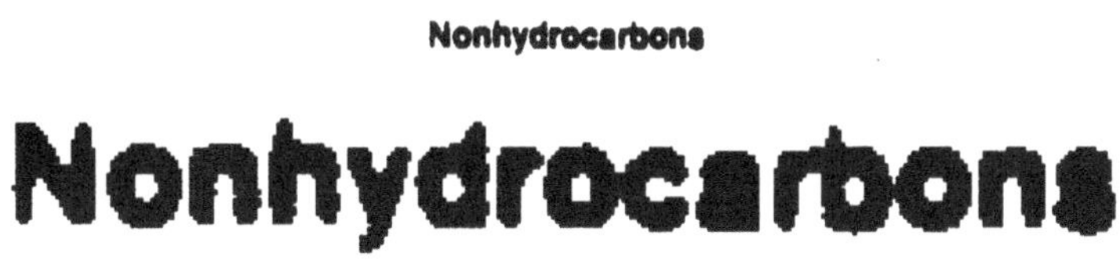

Nonhydrocarbons

Nonhydrocarbons
Nonhydrocarbona
Nenhydrecartona

A few pixels can make all the difference. Each system recognizes the first `s` in *15*, but only one can identify the second one. Perhaps comparing the two s's would help. Two systems identify the s's in *16*, but the `m` is unmanagable.

2.1 *15*

```
sites

site.
sites
sitea
```

2.1 *16*

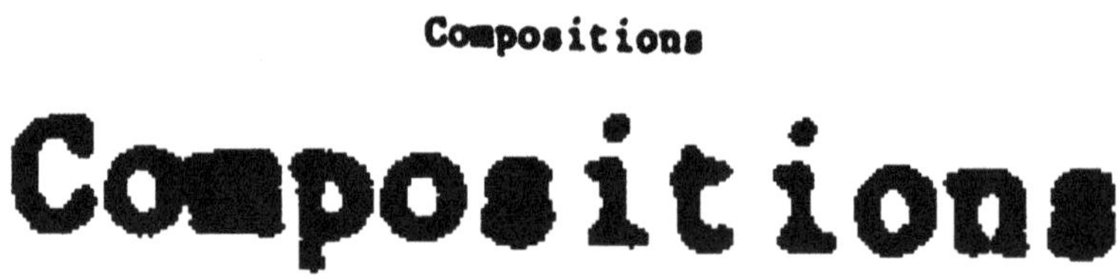

```
Compositions

Co poeitiona
Caapositions
Coupositions
```

The letter **e** is also easily filled, as shown in *15*, *17*, and *18*. The **e** and the **a**'s of *19* are closed yet two systems recognize the first word.

2.1 *17*

```
differences

it/ole
difference:
&I~ur.Ac.u
```

2.1 *18*

```
weight loss

w ight loss
weight loss
w.lght loss
```

2.1 *19*

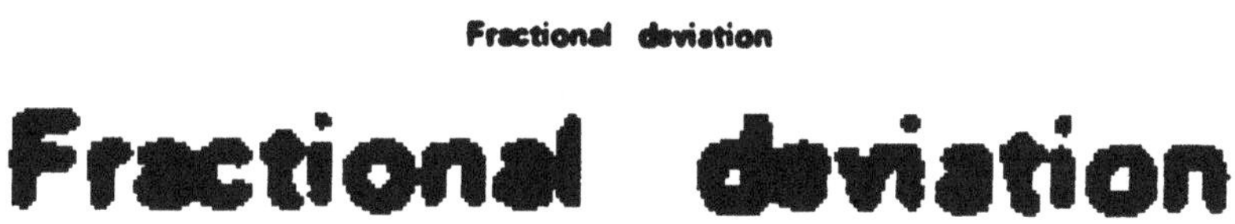


```
Fractional deviation

Fractional dariadon
Fmiaansi aavinion
Fractional diviation
```

A touching rn pair is easily mistaken for an m. Examples are shown in *20*, *21*, and *22*. The non-uniform spacing of the vertical strokes is an important clue. Device 3 is able to separate each of these pairs.

2.1 *20*

Westem

Westem

Western

Westem
Westem
Western

2.1 *21*

McGovem

McGovem

McGovern

McGovem
McGovem
McGovern

2.1 *22*

From Joumal

From Joumal

From Journal

From Joumal
From loumal
From Journal

Similarly, a touching rm resembles nn and rrn. Examples are given in

23, *24*, and *25*. A lexicon can be a valuable tool for resolving the ambiguity. Although permeabilities might not be in the lexicon, term and Form surely are. Unfortunately, so are tern, Fore, and torn.

2.1 *23*

long-term

long-term

long-term

long-term
long-tenn
long-tern

2.1 *24*

Waste Form

Waste Form

Waste Form

Waste Fore
Waste torn
Waste 70Th

2.1 *25*

permeabilities

permeabilities

permeabilities

permeabilities
perrneabilities
penneabilities

Heavy print complicates the recognition of condensed type, which has tall, narrow characters designed to save space. Examples are given in *26* and *27*.

2.1 *26*

look for fall, far left:

look for fall, far left:

look for fall, far left:

leek tar fail, tar lent
look for fall, far left:
10.51 ftr fril, f~ loft:

2.1 *27*

simplified

simplified

simplified

simpililed
slmplll'lerl
simplmod

The word in *27* illustrates how an i can resemble an l when its dot and stem are touching. More examples are given in *28*, *29*, *30*, and *31*.

2.1 *28*

functions.

functlons.

functions.

funcUons.
functlons.
functions.

2.1 *29*

Minister Andrei

Minister Andrei

Minister Andrei

Minister Andrei
Minister Andrel
Minister Andrel

2.1 *30*

values In sllver

values In sllver

values in silver

values In sliver
values In sllver
values in silver

2.1 *31*

Diagrammatic

Diagrammatic

Diagrammatic

Dlrammatlc
Diagrammatic
Diagnmmatlc

The systems cannot decipher the heavy print in *32* and *33*, but a human reader is not stumped.

2.1 *32*

Number

Number

Number

Buds
He-her
I&p

2.1 *33*

of some magnitude.

of some magnitude.

of some magnitude.

efaame _
of some nngnīiaide.
(~awLe ~dL

Since the size of the scanning spot and the scanning resolution are fixed, small characters suffer more than large ones. The smallest detail discernible in the image is the size of a pixel, which is a larger proportion of a small character than a large one. Ideally, smaller characters would be scanned with a smaller spot and higher sampling rate. The systems struggle with various parts of *34* and *35*. Very small print is discussed further in Section 5.7.

2.1 *34*

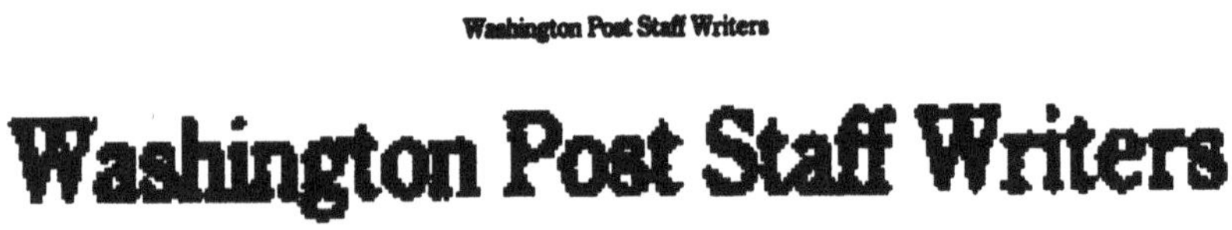


```
Washington Post Staff Writers

Win Post Staff Wit
Washington Poststagwriters
Wmbington Post Staff Writers
```

2.1 *35*

```
time-stratigraphy:

timasrrorigrophy:
time-itratigraphy:
h.me-stratigraph~:
```

2.2 Light Print

It is the consensus of OCR experts that light, fragmented characters cause more errors than heavy, blurred characters. This may be a natural consequence of the fact that there are generally more white pixels, even in text areas of the page, than black pixels. Therefore, converting a black pixel to a white pixel loses more information than vice versa.

Light print may be due to weak-fingered typists, misadjusted impact printers, worn ribbons, tired printer or copier cartridges, or an inadequate scanning threshold.

In extreme cases, only a few pixels of a character remain, not even enough for a human to identify the character in isolation. This is the case for the C in *01*, the first e in *02*, and the 1 in *03*.

2.2 *01*

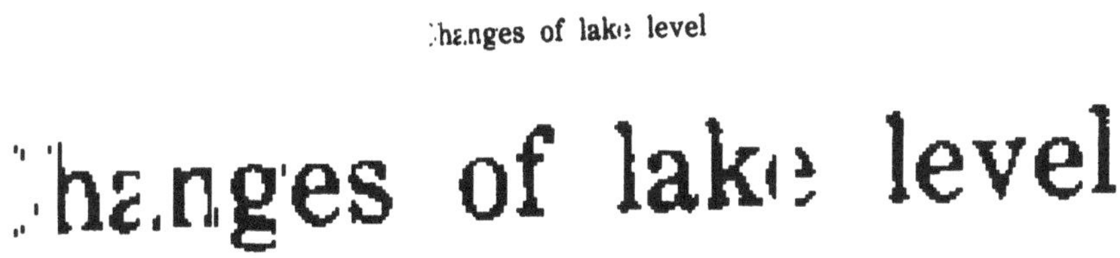

```
Changes of lake level

wages of lake level
~he.n~g~es of lake level
n~.nges of lake.' leve]
```

2.2 *02*

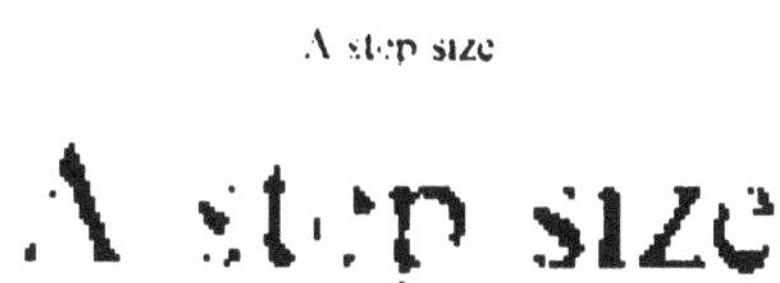

```
A step size

.\ n size
.\ xtvn size
.\ .t p ,iz~
```

2.2 *03*

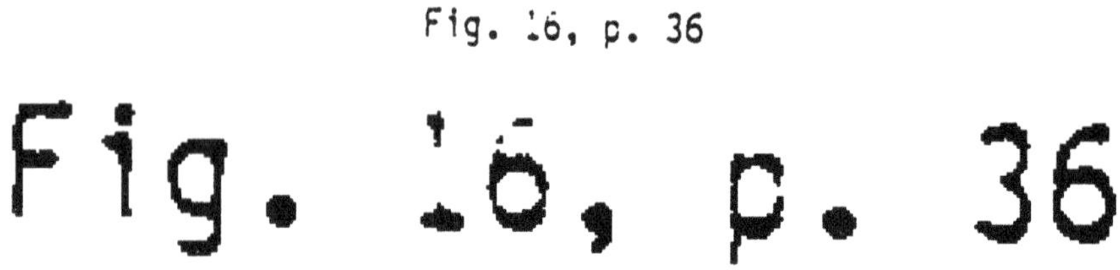

Fig. 16, p. 36

Fig. Lo, p. 36
Fig. Lo, p. 35
Fig. '0<, p. 35

Excessive fragmentation may destroy an entire phrase, as in *04*, *05*, and *06*. The systems cannot handle such degradation and they produce gibberish as a result.

2.2 *04*

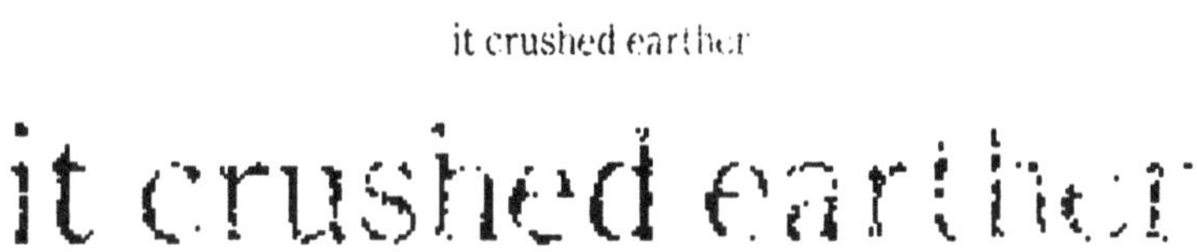

it crushed earthen

it c from d e ii r . at.
it t~ri~isiie<i ~
t cri~s~i,'(1 ('F,'

2.2	05

Alameda, CA 94501-1095

Alameda, CA 94501-1095

Alameda, CA 94501-1095

- amens CA 9460' 'A
Aameaa CA 9450i~iZ$E
amana uA aa~

2.2	06

Imaging Experts

Imaging Experts

Imaging Experts

lE('GjL1\4 LNI)f\1`
lnmgiru; Lxpruis
Iiiij~in~ L\1)(4~

It is difficult for an OCR system to determine which fragment belongs to which character. Fine strokes in italics are easily broken, as shown in *07* and *08*. Italics are difficult to recognize even without defects, and are discussed further in Section 5.1.

2.2 *07*

A Not-For Pr ?fit Organ:zation

A Not-For Pr ?fit Organ:zation

```
A Not-For Profit Organization

iVot-For Al ,/,/ ()r`:fn Fin
~ {lrjuzln zuljbn
t VoI-Foj ?/f! ()r{'.9n
```

2.2 *08*

General Manager

General :Manager

```
General Manager

Ge??e?'al .`lan`?ye?
Ceneruj ~`lunugw~
Ge~iera/ ~Idflc/~p
```

Broken characters give rise to curious misinterpretations in *09*. The isolated stems of the b and h are recognized as l's, and the slightly curved remainder of the h is identified as a z by Device 2. Device 3 fails to connect the two pieces of the a, and generates a t for the right-hand piece despite its evident dissimilarity from the real t nearby.

2.2 **09**

Saltbush.

Saltbush.

```
Saltbush.

Salthusln
Saltlmslz.
S(tlt.bush.
```

The systems struggle to identify broken uppercase letters in *10*, *11*, *12*, and *13*. Notice the lack of uniformity in the fragmentation, for example, the splintered **TIMBER** near the solid **MOUNTAIN** in *13*.

2.2 **10**

OIL SHALE

OIL SHALE

```
OIL SHALE

OLL SIIAI.I
O LL SHAL!5
OLL SIIAI-E
```

2.2 *11*

SOUTH CENTRAL

SOUTH CENTRAL

SOUTH CENTRAL

SOT, :: CENTRAL
some ~cH~N~rRAL
S')~ Cl'NI'RAL

2.2 *12*

VOLCANIC

VOLCANIC

VOLCANIC

I, '.A-NIC
v;~I,~;ANIc
1< YANIC

2.2 *13*

TIMBER MOUNTAIN

TIMBER MOUNTAIN

TIMBER MOUNTAIN

T EMBER MOUNTAIN
rumen MOUNTAIN
T'AiBER MOUNTAIN

The examples in *14* and *15* show that a split H is easily transformed into l's. In *15*, the presence of a few more pixels in the crossbar of the first H helps Device 2 to recognize it.

2.2 *14*

Haley (1960).

Haley (1960).

```
Haley (1960).

ll.ilcy (19(i()).
llttley (l9(i0).
1 I;tlo 5 (1960)
```

2.2 *15*

Howard R.Hughes

Howard R.Hughes

```
Howard R.Hughes

t-loward R.llughes
Howard ltllughes
~loword P,f lughes
```

In *2.1-11* and *2.1-12* on page 16, we saw examples of missegmented touching L's, where the stem was interpreted as an I or an l. Broken-off stems in L's caused by light printing are shown in *16* and *17*.

2.2 *16*

Life

Life

I,ife
Life
I~ife

2.2 *17*

Las Vegas

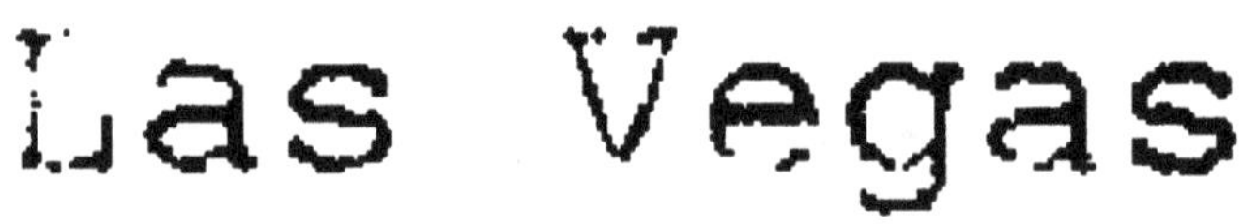

Las Vegas

jam Vegas
has Vegas
.~as Vegas

The examples in *18* and *19* demonstrate how breaks along a vertical line can give rise to a profusion of generated parentheses. More vertical splits appear in *20*. One cannot help admiring Device 2 for getting the entire `route to Tonopah` correct. In *21*, Device 3 produces a plethora of digits for the word `should`.

2.2 *18*

85(X)-milc

8500-mile

8500-mile

85()()-milc
85()()-mile
851)0-mile

2.2 *19*

L. D. Gordon

L. D. Gordon

L. D. Gordon

L. 1). (pardon
L. I). (lordon
L. 1). C~ordon

2.2 *20*

route to Tonopah

route to Tonopah

route to Tonopah

rants tl,’I’onopah
route to Tonopah
i’tiiiti’ to Timotiali

2.2 *21*

plots should be read

plots should be read

plots should be read

plots sloultl be read
plots should be read
plots 11110111(1 be read

In *22*, the horizontal splits in the i and n of function trouble two systems. In *23*, Device 1 correctly identifies the diagonally-broken z, but surprisingly converts the well-formed o to a u. Perhaps Schultz, a more common name, is in its lexicon.

2.2 *22*

as a function

as a function

as a function

as a funct,or,
as a function
as a funct~or~

2.2 *23*

Scholtz

Scholtz

Scholtz

Schultz
Scholt:
Scholt:

Among lowercase letters, e is most vulnerable to confusion with c because in many typefaces the delicate central stroke of the e disappears easily. Such confusions are shown in *24*, *25*, *26*, and *27*. Device 1 must be under the influence of its lexicon when it chooses Cables for pebbles in *27*; however, it correctly recognizes the rare word, desuperposition, in *25*.

2.2 *24*

dcconiposition

dcconiposition

decomposition

dccomposition
dccontposition
decomposition

2.2 *25*

drsuprrpusition

drsuprrpusition

desuperposition

desuperposition
drsuprrpusmon
dcsupcrpusirron

2.2	*26*

claylikc

claylikc

claylike

claylikc
claylikc
claylike

2.2	*27*

pcbbles

pcbbles

pebbles

Cables
pcbbles
pchhles

Because horizontal strokes are often designed to be thinner than vertical strokes, they break more easily. This effect is exaggerated in the typefaces of *28* and *29*.

2.2 *28*

Garth Brooks

Garth Brooks

Garth Brooks

Carlh Block`,
Can-th Brooks
G~irth Llrook~

2.2 *29*

southeru Maryland

southeru Maryland

southern MaryLand

stiuLIIeLu LiLLyL:LiLt]
suutheru nfaryLand
soutLierti MiryLand

Type designers often make loops thinner at the point where they join a thick vertical stroke. A resulting broken d may be interpreted as cl, as in *30*.

2.2	*30*

direct-dialed,

direct-dialed,

```
direct-dialed,

cliret-cli.lel,
direct-dialed.
direct-cliajeti
```

Diagonal strokes tend to be asymmetrical, with NW-SE strokes heavier than NE-SW strokes. This is well illustrated in *31*, *32*, and *33*. The descender of a y is often separated from the rest, and the right-hand stroke of a v must be reported missing.

2.2 *31*

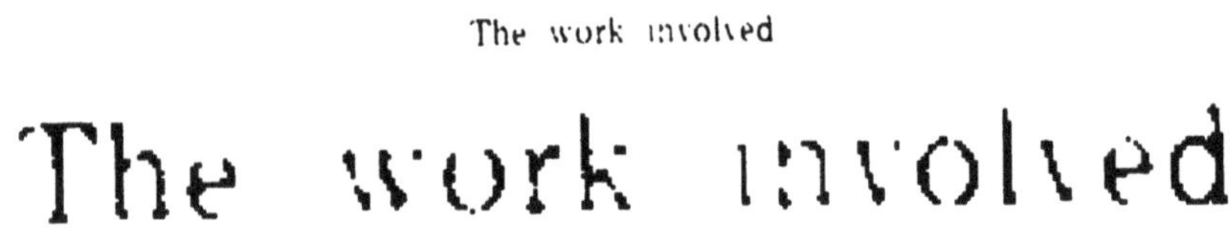

The work involved

The Note m\oL\ed
The work intoLted
The ~,vIIrk In OC\ ~d

2.2 *32*

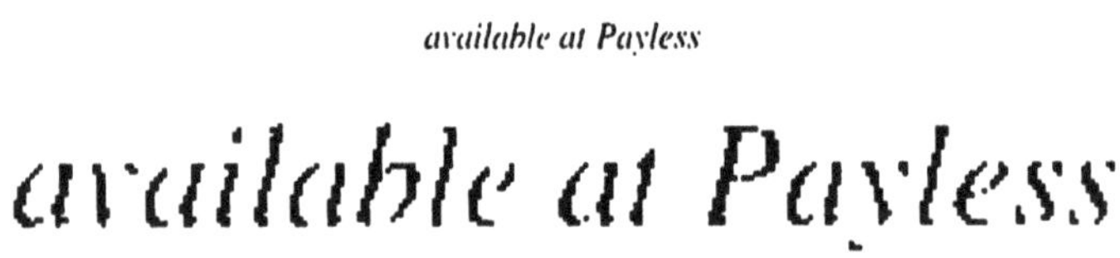

avaiLabLe at PayLess

o-'iLohLc (1 Pt,!k,`..
uruiLaLvLt' at ~
0 (1iL(1I)L(' 0 PijvItyi

2.2 *33*

State University

.`i.re ti:cr`
State L~ni\ ersttv
At ~*fL\ ~r~it\

In *34*, the d has lost its ascender, causing two systems to view it as an o. When an h loses its ascender, it poses as an n, as shown in *35*.

2.2 *34*

Registered

:,egistereo
Registered
?`egistereo

2.2 *35*

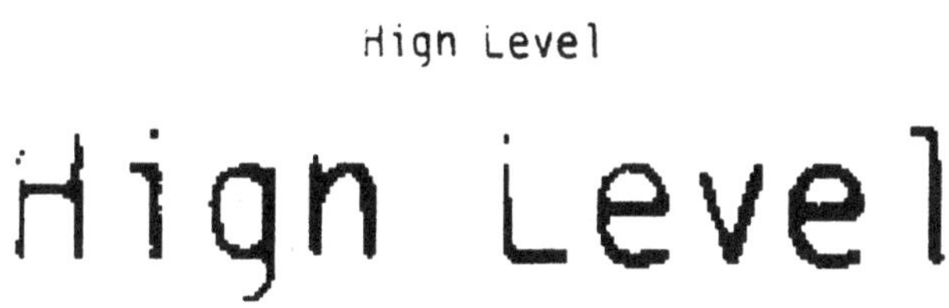

High Level

Sign Level
nign Level
hiqn Level

2.3 Heavy and Light Print

Thin and fat strokes may be near one another within a word or even within a single character. This can be observed on poorly printed or copied pages. Broken and touching characters will co-exist when a dark copy is made from a light copy, or vice versa.

In *01*, the second s is broken and the bottom loop of the g is missing although mog is joined. In *02*, the first letter of the smudged phrase is barely visible. There are some surprising breaks in the hefty strokes of *03*.

2.3 *01*

seismograph

seismograph
seiomoqraph
seiDmoqraph

2.3 *02*

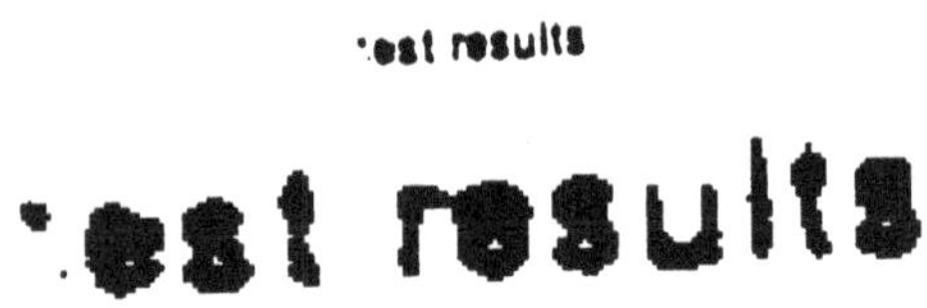

test results

est results
‛eat results
est rasults

In *04* and *05*, the vertical strokes of the **N**'s are much thinner than their diagonals. Each **E** in *05* is closed at the top forming an unexpected loop.

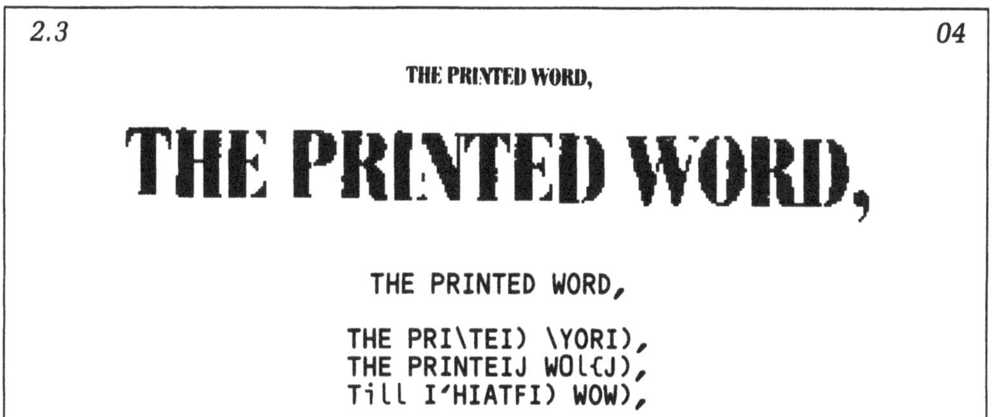

Broken and touching italics appear together in *06*, *07*, and *08*, causing much confusion.

2.3 *06*

private gifts supporting

private gifts supporting

```
private gifts supporting

private gilds suppOni,g
private gm.; supponirig
prii'ate gifts supportbig
```

2.3 *07*

Northwestern University

Northwestern University

```
Northwestern University

Vorthzste. in l.'ruzrsity
Nmlhwr/stem Ijniwriity
\~rlhz~siem t~iii~'ee,j~
```

2.3 *08*

Office of Membership

Office of Membership

```
Office of Membership

Ounce of.llembership
Ojjice ojllernlzersbtp
Offict ofUemI~ersbtp
```

2.4 Stray Marks

Stray marks are a distraction to the OCR process. They are often caused by low-quality print or coarse paper (such as newsprint), but even high-quality typeset material is not immune. Although stray marks can usually be traced to the scanned hard copy, they can also be introduced by specks of dirt on the platen of the scanner, by reflections from the reverse side of the page (optical bleed-through), or by electronic noise on the thresholding circuits. Cheap bond paper often exhibits minuscule black specks. Poorly-maintained copiers may leave extensive smudges. In both *01* and *02*, a stray mark intersects the `t` and interferes with recognition. In *03*, a stray mark between `to` and `live` is interpreted as a character.

2.4 *01*

```
Great Lakes

Grear Lakes
Great Lakes
Grear Lakes
```

2.4 *02*

```
tanks

hanks
tfanks
i:anks
```

2.4	*03*

easy to·live with.

easy to·live with.

easy to live with.

easy torlive with.
easy torlive with.
easy to'live with.

Multiple stray marks, such as those in *04* and *05*, can disorient an OCR system. In *06*, an entire word is obliterated. Stray marks often accompany other defects, such as heavy and light print, as in *07*.

2.4	*04*

;,Young

;,Young

Young

,,Ygung
axoung
~Ypung

2.4 *05*

found

\- found
~foisnd~
fou;nd

2.4 *06*

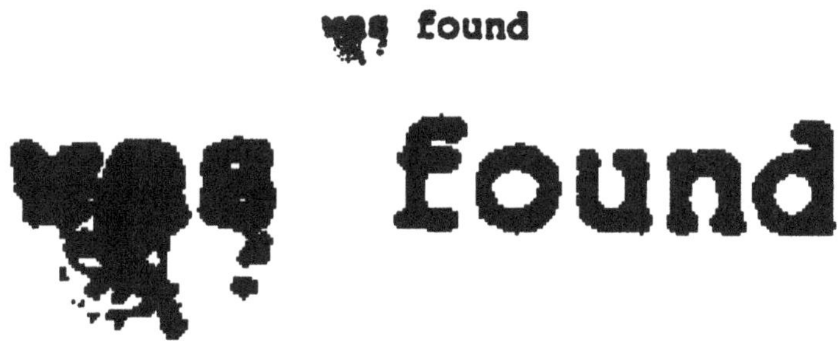

was found

‘ found
Egg found
found

2.4 *07*

```
Nye County

Nge ('ouch
Njje Count?`
Nyc couue~
```

Stray marks are not always so brutish. In *08* and *09*, small and seemingly innocuous specks cause a surprising amount of confusion. Device 1 in particular is working overtime to find an acceptable word from its lexicon. Strangely, it produces a meaningful phrase, `witty verse`, for *08*.

2.4 *08*

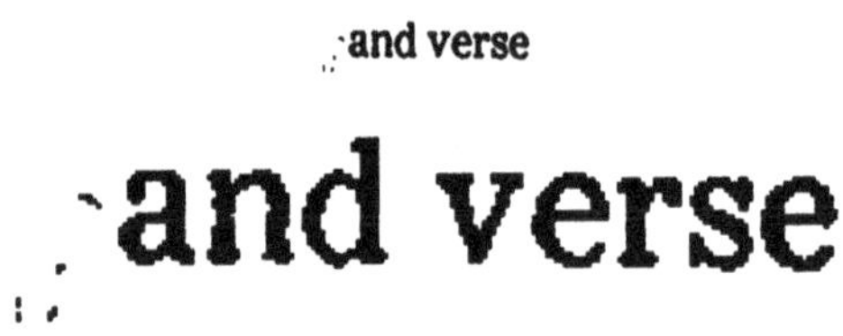


```
and verse

witty verse
xand verse
and verse
```

2.4 *09*

It can .be seen

It can .be seen

It can be seen

It canine seen
It can.be seen
It can ~e seen

The preceding two examples show that stray marks do not have to overlap characters to be troublesome. In *10* and *11*, stray marks occur below the baseline. Interestingly, Device 1 has no trouble with these.

2.4 *10*

have

have

have

have
havie
hays

2.4 *11*

cholesterol

cholesterol

choLesteroL

choLesteroL
choLestero~L
choLesteroJ

Indeed, a minute stray mark positioned in the right way can lead an OCR system astray. In *12*, an errant dot convinces all three systems that the right-hand half of the quotation mark is a question mark. In *13*, two systems are fooled into believing that the `w` is uppercase.

2.4 *12*

both.”

both."

both.‘?
both.‘?
both.‘?

2.4 *13*

will

will

will
Will
Will

Many kinds of stray marks can appear on the hard-copy original. A reader may have circled or underlined a passage of text by hand, as in *14*. Handwritten strokes from a signature overlap the text in *15*. Portions of a stamp applied to the hard copy are visible in *16*, but `ruby r fiction` is a surprising interpretation. A small hole in the paper is responsible for the defect between the **N** and **T** of *17*.

2.4 *14*

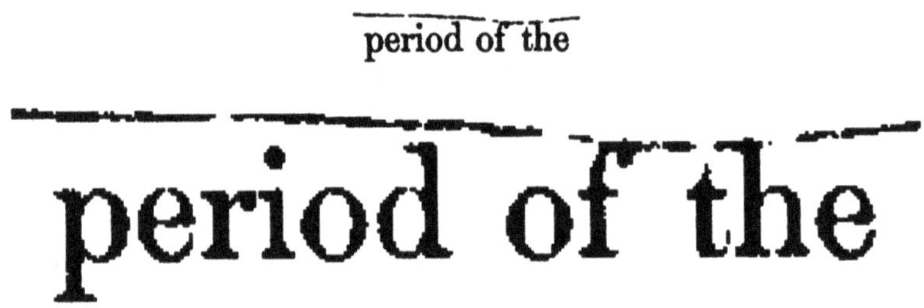

period of the

period o-f-te

periJdTh~~e

2.4 *15*

Sincerely,

(inc5l44
iincetgx
<nil>

2.4 *16*

subscription

ruby r fiction
gubwprbgtion
ub cr tion

2.4 *17*

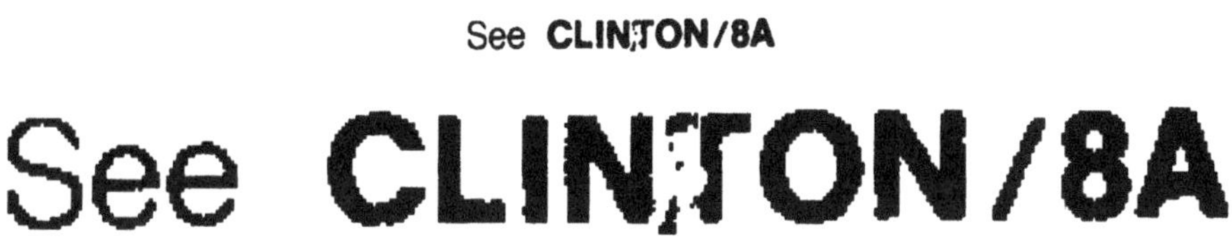

See CLINTON/8A

See CLINTON /8A
See CLINIION/8A
See CLIN;fONI8A

2.5 Curved Baselines

Photocopying or scanning a page of a bound book creates curved baselines. The following figure illustrates how the location of a line affects its appearance. A line near the top of a left-hand page (a) finishes in a downward direction, whereas a line near the bottom (b) ends by swerving upward. For a right-hand page, a line near the top (c) starts in an upward direction before leveling off, whereas a line near the bottom (d) begins by sloping downward.

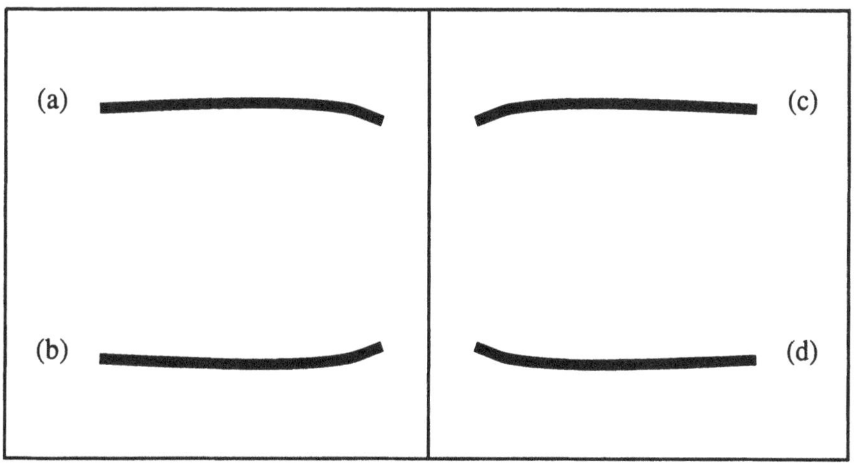

Examples of these four types of curved baselines are shown in *01*, *02*, *03*, and *04*. The characters nearest the binding are the most distorted. They are out of focus, lose their shape and often touch their neighbors. Furthermore, stray marks are frequently present.

2.5 *01*

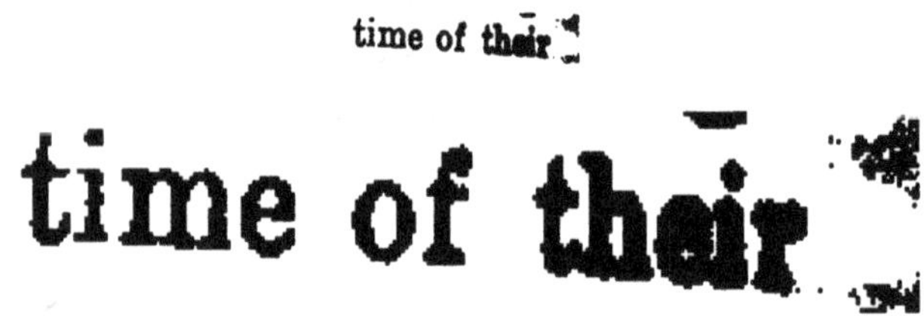

```
time of their

time of :,=7'
time of theirf
time of thm!~
```

2.5 *02*

```
van OLphen

van OLpLibo
van OLpLten
van OLpbefL
```

2.5 *03*

extend his appreciation

extend his appreciation

extend his appreciation

blend his appreciation
(trend his appreciation
e~tend his appreciation

2.5 *04*

Twelve wells

Twelve wells

Twelve wells

twelve wells
Twelve wells
~elve wells

The examples in *05* and *06* show how difficult it can be to identify distorted characters on a curved baseline. Neighboring lines intrude in *06*.

2.5 *05*

movement

sent
LM~em.nt
~

2.5 *06*

before publication

ore gubliatioo
hum publication
~ publiCitiOL

Chapter 3

Similar Symbols

Things either are what they appear to be; or they neither are, nor appear to be; or they are, and do not appear to be; or they are not, and yet appear to be. Rightly to aim in all these cases is the wise man's task.

— from the *Discourses of Epictetus*, circa 100 A.D.

Some symbols look so similar that they are difficult to distinguish even when they are cleanly printed and suffer no imaging defects. Contextual methods are needed to resolve the ambiguity. For example, if an unknown symbol is tall and circular, it could be the numeral 0 or the letter O. But if an adjacent character is a digit, it is more likely to be a zero. Choosing among 1, l, and I for an unknown vertical symbol is especially difficult, and is the topic of Section 3.1. In Section 3.2, we consider 0 and O, and other confusing pairs.

3.1 Similar Vertical Symbols

The symbols, 1, l, and I, are very similar in appearance and sometimes identical. For example, on many older typewriters, the same key is pressed to type a 1 or an l (e.g., `1 liter`). In a sans serif typeface such as Helvetica, the l and I may be indistinguishable (e.g., Illinois). OCR systems (and humans) must rely on context to identify these characters.

A good rule of thumb is that digits appear with other digits and letters appear with other letters. Exceptions to this rule, such as **Part #A150G** and **Waterloo, Ontario N2J 4M1**, are relatively uncommon. If an unknown vertical symbol appears beside a digit, then it is reasonable to assume that it is a 1. If it is next to a letter, then it is probably an l or an I. Unless the entire word is in uppercase, a vertical symbol found in the middle or at the end of a word is likely to be an l. When the vertical symbol is the first letter of a word, a lexicon can be used to decide whether it is an l or an I. For example, lion and India are words, but not Iion or lndia.

Using this strategy, when the **9** in *01* is identified, the vertical symbol to its left should be declared a 1. Similarly, if the **8** in *02* is recognized correctly, then the 1 to its right should be properly identified. Device 1 believes this **8** is a letter (X), which may have influenced its choice of I for the vertical stroke.

3.1 *01*

1968

1968

1968

1968
l968
l968

3.1 *02*

He was 81.

He was 81.

He was 81.

He was X I.
He was 8l.
He was 81.

In *03* and *04*, the sans serif I is puzzling to the OCR systems. Although each system correctly determines that the vertical symbol is a letter, the choice of letter is unclear. The word Inyo is probably not in their lexicon. Although the American National Standards Institute is well known, its acronym might not be part of a lexicon.

3.1 *03*

Wh Ite-Inyo

Wh Ite-Inyo

White-Inyo

White-Layo
white-Lnyo
White-Lnyo

3.1 *04*

ANSI/ASME

ANSI/ASME

ANSI/ASME

ANSi/ASME
ANSL/ASME
ANSIJASME

The 1 in *05* is misinterpreted by two systems, but all three systems correctly identify the abbreviation for pound, lb. In this case, the vertical symbol is next to a letter (b), and lb, but not Ib, could be in the lexicon. However, this logic gives the wrong result in *06*! The strategy is undermined when a digit neighbors a letter. A 1 appears among letters in *07*. The I in *08* precedes two digits.

3.1 *05*

1/4-lb.

1/4-lb.

1/4-lb.

I /4-lb.
l/4-lb.
1/4-lb.

3.1 06

Fig. lb.

Fig. lb.

Fig. 1b.

Fig. lb.
Fig. lb.
Fig. lb.

3.1 07

Proc. 1st Cong.

Proc. 1st Cong.

Proc. 1st Cong.

Proc. I st Cong.
Proc. I st Cong.
Proc. 1st Cong.

3.1 08

I-57: Left lane

I-57: Left lane

I-57: Left lane

1-57: Left lane
I-57: Left lane
1-57: Left lane

If a vertical symbol stands alone, it is safe to assume that it is not an l. But a difficult choice must be made between 1 and I. In *09* and *10*, the solitary vertical stroke is a 1; in *11* and *12*, it is an I.

3.1 *09*

1 percent level

1 percent level

```
1 percent level

I percent level
l percent level
1 percent level
```

3.1 *10*

less than 1 meter

less than 1 meter

```
less than 1 meter

less than I meter
less than l meter
less than 1 meter
```

3.1 *11*

I have learned

I have learned

```
I have learned

l have learned
l have learned
I have learned
```

3.1 *12*

Langmuir, I.

Langmuir, I.

```
Langmuir, I.

Langmuir, 1.
Langmuir, l.
Langmuir, 1.
```

The OCR systems face the same dilemma when they encounter an isolated pair of vertical symbols. Each symbol might be an Arabic 1 as in *13*, or a Roman I as in *14*.

3.1 **13**

11 grams;

11 grams;

```
11 grams;

I I grams;
l l grams;
II grams;
```

3.1 **14**

Ghostbusters II

Ghostbusters II

```
Ghostbusters II

Ghostbusters 11
Ghostbusters [1
Ghostbusters II
```

Device 2 produces a left bracket (`[`) for an `I` in *14* and a right bracket (`]`) for the `1` in *15*. Brackets are two more vertical symbols to contend with; examples are shown in *16*.

3.1 *15*

19th-century

19th-century

19th-century

19th-century
]9th-century
J9th-centu~y

3.1 *16*

[6]

[6]

[6]

61
IS}
16]

In *07*, *14*, and *15*, we see that vertical symbols may be slanted. This means that the slash symbol (/) is another source of confusion, as illustrated by *17*. In *18*, the 1 is slanted enough for Device 1 to interpret it as a 7.

3.1 *17*

up to 60 m/s,

up to 60 m/s,

up to 60 m/s,

up to 60 m/s,
up to 60 ml s,
up to 60 mIs,

3.1 *18*

1.2 million

1.2 million

1.2 million

7.2 million
l.2 million
1.2 million

In some typefaces, the letter J differs little from a vertical stroke. Examples are given in *19* and *20*.

3.1 *19*

Penrose, R. A. F., Jr.

Penrose, R. A. F., Jr.

Penrose, R. A. F., Jr.

Penrose, R. A. F., Jr.
Penrose. R. A. F.. Lr.
Penrose, R. A. F.. Ir.

3.1 *20*

San Jacinto

San Jacinto

San Jacinto

San Lacinto
San jacinto
San jacinto

The letter `i` is confused with `l` in the following examples, which illustrate the overzealous use of a lexicon. In *21*, the well-formed `i` in `Heim` is disregarded by two systems who prefer `Helm`. In *22*, `Alien` is chosen by two systems in lieu of `Allen`.

3.1 *21*

Dr. Albrecht Heim,

Dr. Albrecht Heim,

```
Dr. Albrecht Heim,

Dr. Albrecht Helm,
Dr. Allirecht Heim,
Dr. AIl)recht Helm,
```

3.1 *22*

my husband, Allen,

my husband, Allen,

```
my husband, Allen,

my husband,Alien,
myhusband, Alien,
my husband, Allen,
```

SLEEZY★NEWS
EXCLUSIVE
"MY HUSBAND, ALIEN"

3.2 Other Similar Symbols

In this section, we consider other symbols that are hard to distinguish. We begin with the numeral 0 and the letter O, which are among the most difficult, and then illustrate other confusing pairs.

By checking whether neighboring characters are digits or letters, an unknown circular symbol can be identified. Using this technique, the O in PO and the 0 in 10864 can be recognized correctly in *01*; however, two systems generate P0 instead of PO. In *02*, the zero in the zip code can be identified only after determining that the vertical strokes on either side are digits.

3.2 *01*

PO Box 10864

PO Box 10864

PO Box 10864

PO Box 10864
P0 Box 10864
P0 Box 10864

3.2 *02*

89101

89101

89101

89101
89l0l
89101

In *03*, the s in the abbreviation for thousands, **1000s**, convinces two systems that the circular symbols must be letters. Device 3 even tries to make a word out of it. Indeed, it is very difficult to identify ambiguous shapes in a mixed sequence of letters and digits, as in *04*.

3.2 *03*

1000s

1000s

1000s

L000s
L000s
b00s

3.2 *04*

1OCFR960

1OCFR960

10CFR960

tOCFR960
10CFR960
LOCFR960

There are other rotund symbols that can be confused. In *05*, the **Q** is perceived to be an **O** by two systems. In *06*, two systems believe the isolated **D** is a zero.

3.2 *05*

Quaternary

Quaternary

Quaternary

Ouaternary
Quaternary
Ouaternary

3.2 *06*

APPENDIX D

APPENDIX D

APPENDIX D

APPENDIX D
APPENDIX 0
APPENDIX 0

In *07*, the systems have every reason to believe that each zero is a lowercase o. (These are "old style" numerals; see also *5.5-09* on page 150). In *08*, each zero has been printed with a slash through it to distinguish it from the letter 0, but this only seems to confuse two systems.

3.2 *07*

$1,000-a-day

$1,000-a-day

$1,000-a-day

$r,ooo-a-day
$I,ooo-a-day
$i,ooo-a-day

3.2 *08*

Ø2:49:41.Ø

Ø2:49:41.Ø

02:49:41.0

02:49:A1.0
92:49:41.9
~2:49:41.~

In *09*, the a in Nonmedical looks like an o. In *10*, the q resembles a g. A lexicon is unable to help if the word is not in it. Quantitative is probably in most lexicons, but not quantative.

3.2 **09**

Nonmedical

Nonmedical

Nonmedical

Nonmedicol
Nonmedital
Nonmedicol

3.2 **10**

quantative

quantative

quantative

quantative
guantative
guantative

To the OCR systems, the **G** looks like a **C** in *11*, and the **R**'s resemble **B**'s in *12*. In *13*, the systems reference three different figures. A lexicon provides no help for these cases.

3.2 *11*

in G-Tunnel

in G-Tunnel

in G-Tunnel

in C-Tunnel
in G-Tunnel
in C-Tunnel

3.2 *12*

GARRELS

GARRELS

GARRELS

GABBELS
GABRELS
GARRELS

3.2 *13*

FIGURE 26

FIGURE 26

FIGURE 26

FIGURE 26
FIGURE 25
FIGURE 28

The x in *14* bears some resemblance to an r, but a lexicon cannot resolve the matter since it contains both Wax and War. Although the name Bonk is well formed in *15*, two systems prefer the word Bank from their lexicon. Similar over-reliance on a lexicon is evident in *16*, where discontinue is favored over discontinua, and in *17*, where series replaces aeries.

3.2 *14*

Wax plug

Wax plug

Wax plug

War plug
Wax plug
War plug

3.2 *15*

J. Bonk

J. Bonk

J. Bonk

J. Bank
J. Bank
J. Bonk

3.2	*16*

discontinua

discontinua

discontinua

discontinue
discontinue
discontinua

3.2	*17*

glass-enclosed aeries

glass-enclosed aeries

glass-enclosed aeries

glass-enclosed series
glass-enclosed aeries
glassenclosed series

A lexicon does not help to distinguish the uppercase and lowercase forms of a letter. These forms differ only by their size for the following letters: Cc, Oo, Pp, Ss, Uu, Vv, Ww, Xx, and Zz. But in *18*, the uppercase W is only slightly taller than the lowercase letters, thereby confusing all three systems. The case of SMALL CAPS is in doubt in *19*.

3.2 *18*

We've

We've

We've

we've
we`ve
we've

3.2 *19*

THE MAPLE PRESS

THE MAPLE PRESS

THE MAPLE PRESS

THE MAP! E PRESS
THE MAPLE Puss
THE MAPLE PRESs

Generally, a word appears in all uppercase (WOW), all lowercase (wow), or is capitalized (Wow). Other combinations are very rare (WOw, WoW, wOW, wOw, woW). This convention can be used to help distinguish an uppercase letter from its lowercase counterpart. However, when an uppercase letter does appear in the middle of a word, as in *20*, it may be missed. In *21*, all three systems are unprepared for keV, the abbreviation for kilo electron-volts.

3.2 *20*

BookStore.

BookStore.

BookStore.

BookStore.
Bookstore.
Bookstore.

3.2 *21*

74.67 keV

74.67 keV

74.67 keV

74.67 key
74.67 kev
74.67 key

B-8 and S-5 are troublesome pairs. Since one symbol is a letter and the other is a digit, checking the identity of neighboring characters is fruitful. But in the following examples, letters and digits appear together, which foils this method. Given the symbols B and 5 in *22*, Device 1 decides both are letters, while Devices 2 and 3 believe both are digits. The systems have difficulty deciding whether there are B's or 8's in *23*. When an S appears beside a digit in *24*, it is reported to be a 5. Conversely in *25*, a 5 next to a letter must be an S!

3.2 *22*

FIGURE B.5.

FIGURE B.5.

FIGURE B.5.

FIGURE B.S.
FIGURE 8.5.
FIGURE 8.5.

3.2 *23*

B03, B17, B41,

B03, B17, B41,

B03, B17, B41,

803, B17, 841,
803. 817, 841.
B03, B17, 841,

3.2 *24*

37891S

37891S

37891S

378915
378915
37891S

3.2 *25*

well 5C

well 5C

well 5C

well SC
well SC
well SC

Chapter 4

Punctuation

“#@%*!”

— Anonymous

Punctuation symbols serve as guideposts in written material much like inflection and phrasing in speech About 60% of all punctuation symbols are commas and periods, Considering their prevalence. it is unfortunate that they look so similar Their small size prevents type designers from doing much to distinguish them, When an OCR system omits or confuses these symbols. it produces text that is disconcerting to read,

Dashes and hyphens are the next most common symbols, accounting for roughly 15% of all punctuation, with end-of-line hyphens comprising the bulk of these. Quotation marks and apostrophes combine for 10% of the punctuation, parentheses account for 5%, and semicolons and colons together represent another 5%. The remaining 5% is split among the following: exclamation mark (!), question mark (?), number sign (#), dollar sign ($), at sign (@), percent sign (%), ampersand (&), asterisk (*), slash (/), plus (+), less than (<), greater than (>), equal sign (=), brackets ([ ]), and braces ({ }). These percentages vary considerably with the author and type of material; for example, in the *King James Bible* and in Shakespeare’s *First Folio*, more than 10% of the punctuation marks are colons. If we consider all characters excluding spaces, about one in 20 is a punctuation symbol. By contrast, one in 10 is the letter **e**, the most common character.

We are considering only those characters that are part of the ASCII set, but there are many other symbols that may appear on a page. Some OCR systems will recognize some of these: cent (¢), pound (£), yen (¥), bullet (•), section (§), copyright (©), degree (°), multiply (×), and divide (÷). The Spanish language has a couple of its own (¡ ¿), and shares with French, quotations between «comillas/guillemets». A game of bridge may be described using ♠, ♥, ♦, and ♣. Mathematicians depend on arcane notation ($\ni$ $\forall$ $\exists$ $\therefore$ ∂ $\cap$ $\subseteq$) and have pressed into service entire foreign alphabets, including Greek, Gothic, and Hebrew. The European Patent Office reportedly needs more than 500 special symbols to convert its multilingual patent collection to computer-readable form. At one time, typewriters enforced a strict limit on the number of special symbols, but with computerized document-production systems, the possibilities are now endless (✓ ☆ ➤ ☎ ☞). The number of combinations of black and white pixels in a 20 × 20 array is more than one googol (1 followed by 100 zeroes).

We begin our analysis of punctuation with an examination of commas and periods in Section 4.1. Recognizing quotation marks is surprisingly difficult and is the subject of Section 4.2. A sampling of other punctuation symbols is presented in Section 4.3.

4.1 Commas and Periods

Commas are especially prone to misinterpretation. In many typefaces, the tail of the comma is a delicate stroke, and is susceptible to breakage and truncation. When this key differentiating feature is damaged or missing, an OCR system will usually conclude that the comma is a period. Examples are shown in *01*, *02*, and *03*.

4.1 *01*

In consequence. the

In consequence. the

```
In consequence, the

In consequence. the
In consequence. the
In consequence. the
```

4.1 *02*

readings. in terms of

readings. in terms of

```
readings, in terms of

readings. in terms of
readings. in terms of
readings. in terms of
```

4.1 *03*

relief. therefore. is

relief. therefore. is

```
relief, therefore, is

relief. therefore. is
relief. therefore. is
relief. therefore, is
```

Periods occur most often at the end of a sentence and are thus followed by the capitalized first word of the next sentence. On the other hand, commas normally occur within a sentence and are followed by an uncapitalized word. Thus, when an OCR system is unsure whether a symbol is a comma or a period, it can use the case of the next letter as a clue. The three preceding examples yield to this technique; however, an uppercase letter can follow a comma, as in *04* and *05*, so this method is not foolproof. The example in *05* illustrates how heavy print can merge the tail with the head of the comma.

4.1 *04*

his brother. Ronald.

his brother. Ronald.

```
his brother, Ronald,

his brother' Ronald.
his brother. Ronald.
his brother, Ronald.
```

4.1 *05*

Las Vegas, NV

Las Vegas, NV

Las Vegas, NV

Las Vegas. NV
Las Vegas. NV
Las Vegas, NV

An OCR system could contrast ambiguous shapes with symbols that it believes with confidence to be periods. This technique might help to identify the commas in *06* and *07*.

4.1 *06*

U.S. Geological Survey,

U.S. Geological Survey,

U.S. GeoLogicaL Survey,

U.S. Geoioegicai Survey.
U.S. GeoLogicaL Survey.
U.S GeoLogicaL Survey,

4.1 *07*

WASHINGTON, D.C.

WASHINGTON, D.C.

WASHINGTON, D.C.

WASHINGTON D.C.
WASHINGTON. D.C.
WASHINGTON. D.C.

Correctly distinguishing commas from periods is vital when recognizing numbers. In *08*, the value is significantly altered if **4.500** replaces **4,500**. The population of the town described in *09* shrinks drastically.

4.1 *08*

4.500 3,500

4.500 3,500

4,500 3,500

4.500 3,500
4.500 3,500
4.500 3,500

4.1 *09*

4,300 residents

4.300 residents

4,300 residents

4.300 residents
4.300 residents
4.300 residents

SMALLSVILLE
POPULATION 4.3

Like commas and periods, semicolons and colons are easily confused. In both *10* and *11*, the semicolon is identified as a colon.

4.1 *10*

forests;

forests;

forests;

forests:
forests:
forests:

4.1 *11*

layout;

layout;

layout;

layout:
layout;
layout:

Although commas may often be interpreted as periods, a period is seldom identified as a comma. In both *12* and *13* though, the period is misshapen enough for this to occur.

4.1 *12*

MULTIPLIER.

MULTIPLIER.

MULTIPLIER.

MULTIPLIER,
MULTIPLIER.
MULTIPLIER,

4.1 *13*

consideration,

consideration,

consideration.

consideration,
consideration,
consideration,

Sometimes a comma or period is so small and light that it is ignored by an OCR system, that is, no character is generated for it. The system may believe it to be a stray mark. Examples are shown in *14*, *15*, and *16*.

4.1 *14*

8.3.1.17.3

8.3.1.17.3

8.3.1.17.3

8.3.1 17.3
8.3.1~17.3
8.3.1 17.3

4.1 *15*

In response,

In response,

In response,

In response
In response.
In response

4.1 *16*

P.O. Box

P.O. Box

P.0. Box

P 0. Box
P~0~ Box
P.0 Box

An OCR system may fail to locate a comma or period that is *kerned*, that is, placed beneath part of the preceding letter. In *17*, the comma is tucked beneath the preceding y and is missed by all three systems. The period following `Calif` in *18* is similarly ignored. The first period in *19* is kerned and missed, while the second period is recognized correctly. The kerning leads Device 2 to believe that the **P** is an **R**.

4.1 *17*

community,

community,

```
community,

community
communitv
community
```

4.1 *18*

Berkeley, Calif.

Berkeley, Calif.

```
Berkeley, Calif.

Berkeley, Calif
Berkeley Calif
Berkeley, Calif
```

4.1	*19*
P.O. Box	
P.O. Box	
P.O. Box	
PO. Box RO. Box PO. Box	

Two commas and a period are kerned in *20* with mixed results. The comma in *21* is not kerned and is recognized by all three systems; however, the kerned period is missed by two of them. In *22*, two systems believe that the period is part of a colon. Likewise, the comma in *23* appears to Device 3 to be part of a semicolon.

4.1	*20*
busy, busy, busy.	
busy, busy, busy.	
busy, busy, busy.	
busy, busy, busy. busy, busy busy busy, busy, busy	

4.1	21

Linda Blvd.,

Linda Blvd.,

```
Linda Blvd.,

Linda Blvd.,
Linda Blvd,
Linda Blvd,
```

4.1	22

Planner.

Planner.

```
Planner.

Planner.
Planner:
Planne,:
```

4.1	23

Boulder, CO

Boulder, CO

```
Boulder, CO

Boulder, CO
Boulder CO
Boulder; CO
```

Kerned punctuation is usually applied throughout a passage of text; therefore, it should be possible for an OCR system to detect this and allow for it. More difficult than a kerned comma or period is one that touches the preceding letter. Examples are given in *24* and *25*. Device 1 solves these and the four preceding examples of kerning.

4.1 *24*

investigation.

investigation.

```
investigation.

investigation.
investigation
investigation
```

4.1 *25*

and matching hat.

and matching hat.

```
and matching hat.

and matching hat.
and matching hat
and matching hat
```

4.2 Quotation Marks

"Curved" quotation marks have tails that are as easily damaged as the tails of commas. The quotation marks in *01* are not as deformed as those in *02*.

4.2 *01*

"good" or "bad"

"good" or "bad"

"good" or "bad"

```
"good' or "bad"
"good" or "bad"
`~good' or `~bad"
```

4.2 *02*

"kriging."

"kriging."

"kriging."

```
"'Kriging-.
'-kriging.~
*~kriging.'
```

"Vertical" quotation marks are shown in *03* and *04*. The systems believe that the vertical strokes belong to letters or digits.

4.2 *03*

"cold"

"cold"

"coLd"

"coLd"
HcoLdn
t1coLd"

4.2 *04*

subscript "o"

subscript "o"

subscript "o"

subscript no"
subscript non
subscript 110*1

The vertical strokes are most troublesome when they are very close to one another or are touching. This is illustrated by *05*, *06*, *07*, and *08*. However, except for superscripts, few other symbols are positioned entirely above the midline. Although quotation marks usually come in pairs and serve as delimiters, the inch symbol in *08* reminds us that this is not always the case.

4.2 *05*

"birth" and "death"

"birth" and "death"

"birth" and "death"

birth and death
*birthn and *death*
"birth" and "death"

4.2 *06*

"3-D"

"3-D"

"3-D"

83-D'
n3-D'
"3-D"

4.2	07
"silicated" "silicated" "silicated" 'silicates usilicatedu `silicated'	

4.2	08
4-1/2" O.D. 4-1/2" O.D. 4-1/2" O.D. 4-1/2 O.D. 4-1/2* O.O. 4-1/2" O.D.	

"Slanted" quotation marks are shown in *09* and *10*. Devices 2 and 3 are unable to separate r" in *09*.

4.2 *09*

"Power User"

"Power User"

"Power User"

"Power User"
"Power User'
"Power Usef'

4.2 *10*

"To DELIMIT

"To DELIMIT

"TO DELIMIT

TO DELIMIT
HTO DELIMIT
"To DELIMIT

When a quotation appears within a quotation, ‘single quotes’ are normally used to delimit the inner quotation. If both quotations begin or end together, then three strokes will appear in succession, as illustrated by *11* and *12*. The three strokes can be deciphered by adhering to convention: the sequence “‘ can be assumed to be a double quote followed by a single quote, and ’” indicates a single quote preceding a double quote. If vertical strokes are used, as in '", then it is not so simple. However, if the strokes are “ ‘spaced unequally’ ” as in *12*, then this is a valuable " 'clue.' "

4.2 *11*

‘Help!’”

‘Help!’”

`Help!´"

´Help!"´
`Help!"´
`Help!"´

4.2 *12*

for a dog,’” says

for a dog,’ ” says

for a dog,´" says

for a dog,"´ says
for a dog,´ " says
for a dog,"´ says

4.3 Special Symbols

Although special symbols occur infrequently, they should not be overlooked. Correct recognition of these unique shapes is complicated by imaging defects. An asterisk in *01* and an equal sign in *02* are distorted by heavy print. In *03*, a crease in the paper created a horizontal sequence of gaps in the image, yet only the number sign is misinterpreted. In *04*, a hyphen with an unexpected hole is interpreted as a letter by Devices 1 and 2, and is ignored by Device 3.

4.3 *01*

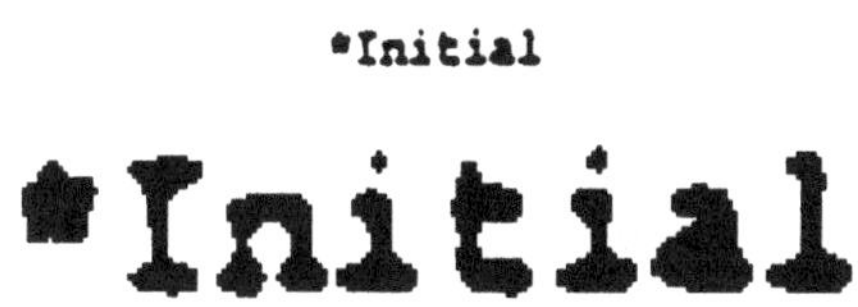

*Initial

.Initia1
'Initial
cInitial

4.3 *02*

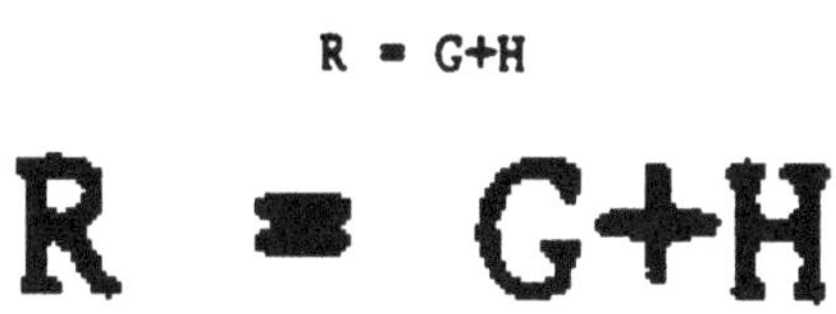

R = G+H

R - G+H
R * G+H
R u G+H

4.3 *03*

Account #

Account #

Account #

Account ,*
Account #
Account ~

4.3 *04*

proper-

proper-

proper-

propero
propera
proper

Even when special symbols are well formed, they can be difficult to distinguish from other characters. To Devices 1 and 2, the ampersand in *05* looks like an **8**, and the dollar sign in *06* appears to be an **S**. In *07*, a symbol that occurs very rarely, the left brace ({), is not recognized by any of the systems.

4.3 *05*

& Conservation

& Conservation

& Conservation

8 Conservation
8 Conservation
& Conservation

4.3 *06*

($6).

($6).

($6).

(S6).
(S6).
($6).

4.3 *07*

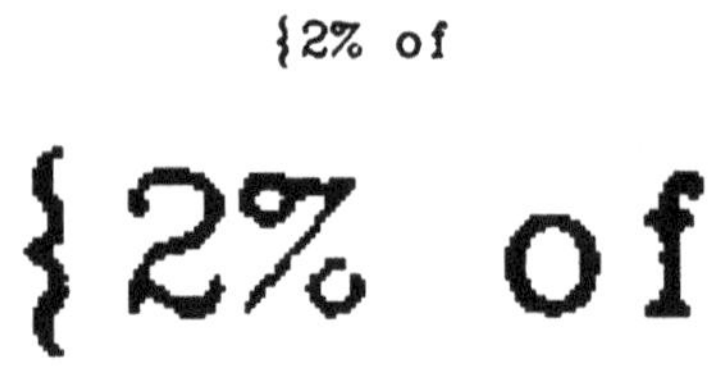

{2% of

270 of
$2% of
~2% of

Possibly, too few of these rare symbols were used to train the OCR systems. There is generally more variation in the shape of special symbols than in that of letters or digits. In *07*, *08*, *09*, and *10*, we see how the appearance of a percent sign can vary due to type design, and heavy and light print.

4.3 *08*

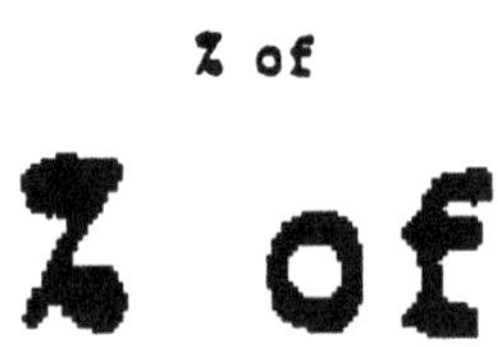

% of

Z of
Z of
% of

4.3 *09*

50‰

50‰

50%

hot
503..
50%

4.3 *10*

71%

71%

71%

71C/c
71%
71~

Chapter 5
Typography

Confusion on thy banners wait.
— from *The Bard* by Thomas Gray, 1757

In this chapter, we consider the problems imposed by the *intended* appearance of text, as opposed to defects that arise in the printing, copying or scanning processes. Responsibility for the final appearance of text is shared by the publisher, editor, graphic designer, typographer, compositor, and printer. In desktop publishing, one person may wear all of these hats.

Typography is the art, or skill, of designing communication by means of the printed word. Good typography is transparent: it reveals rather than hides the message. However, the OCR user normally has no control over the typography and is often faced with layouts, typefaces, and type sizes that are less than ideal for accurate OCR.

Many of today's typefaces have their roots in medieval calligraphy. To imitate fine penmanship, vertical strokes are thick compared to horizontal strokes, and NW-SE diagonals are thicker than NE-SW diagonals. Accordingly, the width of a curved stroke varies as the stroke changes directions. In contrast, typefaces designed specifically for accurate OCR, such as OCR-A and OCR-B, have uniform stroke widths, and exaggerated distinctions between similar symbols, such as 1 and l.

In their heyday, typewriters could be found with any one of several hundred typefaces. There were thousands of different typefaces for letterpress printing. Now a far greater number of digital typefaces are available; furthermore, some desktop publishing software enables users to create even more. The resulting profusion of typefaces provides a continuing challenge for OCR. Here are a variety of typefaces:

Bodoni	abcdefghijklmnopqrstuvwxyz	0123456789
Courier	abcdefghijklmnopqrstuvwxyz	0123456789
Danley	abcdefghijklmnopqrstuvwxyz	0123456789
Ex-Rounded	abcdefghijklmnopqrstuvwxyz	0123456789
Helvetica	abcdefghijklmnopqrstuvwxyz	0123456789
Impact	abcdefghijklmnopqrstuvwxyz	0123456789
Letter	abcdefghijklmnopqrstuvwxyz	0123456789
Madison	abcdefghijklmnopqrstuvwxyz	0123456789
Obloquy	abcdefghijklmnopqrstuvwxyz	0123456789
OCR-A	abcdefghijklmnopqrstuvwxyz	0123456789
OCR-B	abcdefghijklmnopqrstuvwxyz	0123456789
Old English	abcdefghijklmnopqrstuvwxyz	0123456789
Palenque	abcdefghijklmnopqrstuvwxyz	0123456789
Rockwell	abcdefghijklmnopqrstuvwxyz	0123456789
Times	abcdefghijklmnopqrstuvwxyz	0123456789
Univers	abcdefghijklmnopqrstuvwxyz	0123456789
University	abcdefghijklmnopqrstuvwxyz	0123456789
Zanders	abcdefghijklmnopqrstuvwxyz	0123456789

Typefaces are grouped according to whether their symbols have serifs or not (*sans serif*), and whether the horizontal space occupied by each symbol is constant (*fixed pitch*) or variable (*proportional pitch*). Courier and Letter are fixed-pitch typefaces, although Courier has serifs and Letter is sans serif. Times and Helvetica are proportional-pitch typefaces, but Times has serifs and Helvetica does not.

A typeface often has several variations or *styles*. Here are several styles of the Bodoni typeface:

	Normal	Bold	Italic	Bold Italic
Bodoni	abcdefg	**abcdefg**	*abcdefg*	***abcdefg***
Bodoni Condensed	abcdefg	**abcdefg**	*abcdefg*	***abcdefg***

Type size is measured in "printer's points" where one point is equal to 1/72 of an inch. Here are several type sizes for Bodoni:

4-point 5-point 6-point 7-point 8-point 9-point 10-point 11-point 12-point 14-point 16-point

18-point 20-point 22-point 24-point

28-point 32-point 36-point

For greatest legibility, 9- to 12-point type is chosen for text set in paragraphs. Smaller sizes are used for footnotes, and larger sizes for titles and headings. A single typeface-style-size combination, such as *12-point Bodoni Italic*, is known as a *font*.

In this chapter, we examine typographic features that complicate OCR. In Section 5.1, we consider *italics* and problems related to the spacing that separates characters, words, and lines. Underlining is studied in Section 5.2. In Sections 5.3 and 5.4, we look at text printed

on a shaded background and in reverse video.

Section 5.5 is devoted to unusual typefaces. Sections 5.6 and 5.7 consider very large print and very small print, respectively.

5.1 Italics and Spacing

An italic or oblique font is a variation of a normal or "roman" typeface in which upright characters are slanted, and their serifs may be transformed into ornamental flourishes called *finials.* Italics are typically kerned, which can make it difficult for an OCR system to isolate individual characters. The lavish f's in *01* are placed very close together. The curving i and touching f's in *02* confuse two systems. The characters in *03* are less crowded, but the l's and i's sport extravagant finials. Italics are often used to highlight special terms, which are unlikely to appear in a lexicon. *Albicaulis*, and *Pinus longaeva* in *04*, refer to species of plants.

5.1 *01*

Effects:

Effects:

```
Effects:

Effects:
Ejects.`
Eft~cts:
```

5.1 *02*

Cliffhanger.

Cliffhanger.

```
Cliffhanger.

Cliffhanger.
Clzjjhanger.
Cl~flh anger.
```

5.1	03

albicaulis

albicaulis

albicaulis

atbicauZis
albicaulis
a~icaulis

5.1	04

Pinus longaeva

Pinus longaeva

Pinus longaeva

Pinus longtime;
Pjnur /orrgaet/a
Pinus longaeva

The special terms in *05* name an Israeli newspaper. Here the characters are placed so closely that several are touching. A similar example is given in *06*. Of course, kerning is not limited to italics. In *07*, the `Fe` of `Fenimore` is kerned and touching.

5.1 **05**

Yedioth Ahronoth,

Yedioth Ahronoth,

```
Yedioth Ahronoth,

Yedth Ahranth,
Yedtoth Ahmnoth,
Yedioth Ahrnvoth,
```

5.1 **06**

Leaving

Leaving

```
Leaving

Lemma
Leaving
```
<nil>

5.1 *07*

Fenimore

Fenimore

`Fenimore`

```
Fenimore
Flenimore
~nimore
```

Sans serif italics lack the distracting finials. However, the characters in *08* are perhaps too slanted for the systems to decipher. The italics in *09* are slanted less but are closer together. Only one system recognizes the abbreviation for cholesterol.

5.1 *08*

Customer Service

Customer Service

```
Customer Service

CosiomerService
        ~
Customer SO(vfc a
```

5.1 *09*

0 mg chol.

0 mg chol.

```
0 mg chol.

0 mg chat
0 mg chol.
Omg chat
```

The italics in *10* illustrate a variety of problems. It is interesting to note that no space characters are produced by any of the systems to separate the words.

5.1 *10*

Office of the Dean

Office of the Dean

```
Office of the Dean

OffceoftheD=n
0]7IceoftlyeDe6m
Office#theDean
```

While we have examined the spacing (or lack thereof) between characters, we now consider the spacing between words. In *11*, the systems fail to identify the space separating of from financial. The space is deliberately kerned with the f's to create a pleasing appearance, and no vertical line could separate the words. To the OCR systems, this space is too narrow to be an "inter-word" space and is assumed to be an "inter-character" space, for which no space character is produced.

5.1 *11*

fear of financial

fear of financial

fear of financial

fear offinancial
fear ofjinancial
frar offinancial

The following examples show more inter-word spaces that are overlooked, but in non-italic fonts. In *12*, the space between of and a is missed by two systems. In *13*, the space before each j is kerned. In *14*, the space separating just from like is quite narrow. In each case, there is sufficient white space, but the "caliper distance" between upright verticals is small and comparable to the inter-character spacing.

5.1 *12*

quarter of a million

quarter of a million

quarter of a milLion

quarter of a milLion
quarter ofa milLion
quarter ofa miTLion

5.1 *13*

I just got a job

I just got a job

I just got a job

I just got a job
Ijust got a job
Ijust got ajob

5.1 *14*

just like them

just like them

just Like them

justLike them
justLike them
just Like them

We have observed that a lack of space between words can inhibit the generation of the space character. In the following examples, we see what happens when there is inadequate *leading* (the space separating lines). In *15*, descenders from the previous line touch a zip code and interfere with its recognition. In *16*, lines are placed so closely that the descenders from one line reach the ascenders of the next line. The example in *17* shows a kind of "vertical kerning" in which lines are intentionally placed close to one another for a stylish effect.

5.1 *15*

20305 - 1000

20301000
20302 - 100g
2030~1000

5.1 *16*

map of the

map of the
ma o the
mapo the

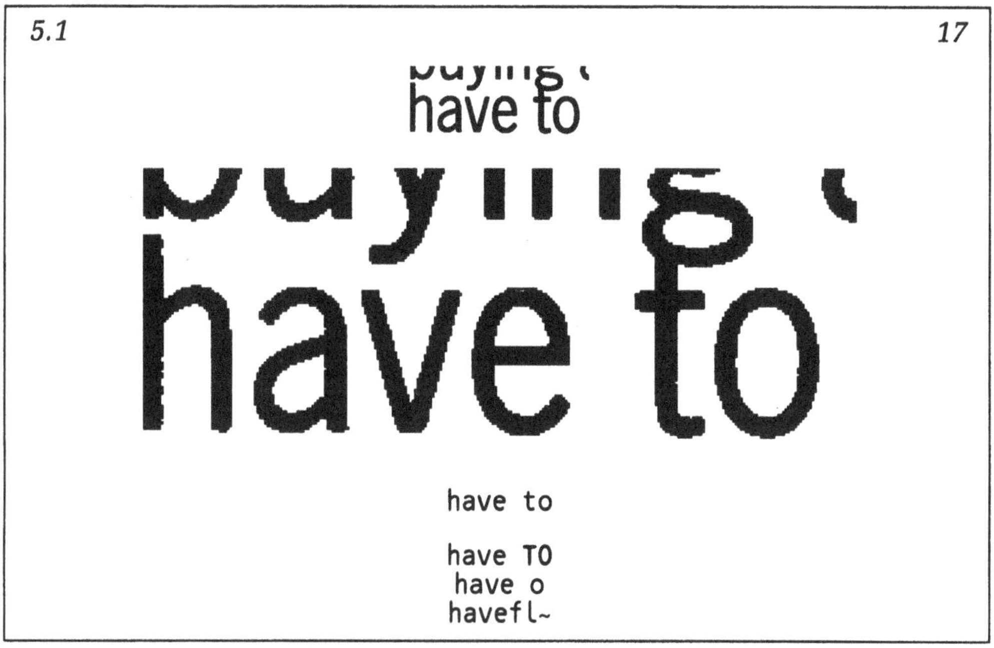
5.1
17
have to
have to
have to
have TO
have o
havefl~

5.2 Underlining

Underlining is used to emphasize words, and in typewritten text, it is used in lieu of italics. To recognize characters that are underlined, an OCR system must separate the characters from the underline. This is especially difficult for characters with descenders that intersect the underline, such as the g's in *01*, the y in *02*, and the p in *03*.

5.2 **01**

bigger

bicker
bigger
biaQer

5.2 **02**

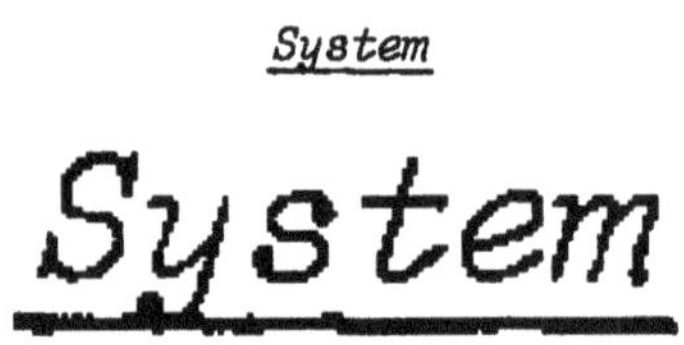

System

Sustem
Sgstem
System

5.2 *03*

Operations

Operations

Operations

ODerations
gperatigns
ODerations

The closer the underline is to the baseline, the more difficult it is to extract the characters. Device 2 is baffled by the close underline in *04*.

5.2 *04*

Congressional

Congressional

Congressional

Conaresslonal
mmmmnimhmngm
Conaressional

In *05*, it is easy to mistake each T for an I. The baseline of *06* is uneven, so only the C's and the I touch the underline.

5.2 *05*

TOTAL

TOTAL

TOTAL

TOTAL
IQIAL
IQIAL

5.2 *06*

CONFIDENCE

CONFIDENCE

CONFIDENCE

CONFIDENT JE
ONE DEN E
CONFIDEN E

Besides underlines, there are other types of lines called *rules* that can interfere with recognition. Rules are used for a variety of design effects including borders, separating lines, and boxes. Footnotes are normally placed beneath a horizontal rule near the bottom of the page. In *07*, a footnote is too close to this line. Horizontal and vertical rules are often used to delineate the rows and columns of a table. In *08*, a character abuts a vertical line and is missed by two systems.

5.2 *07*

*Definitions

definitions
iuefinitions
`tOefinitions

5.2 *08*

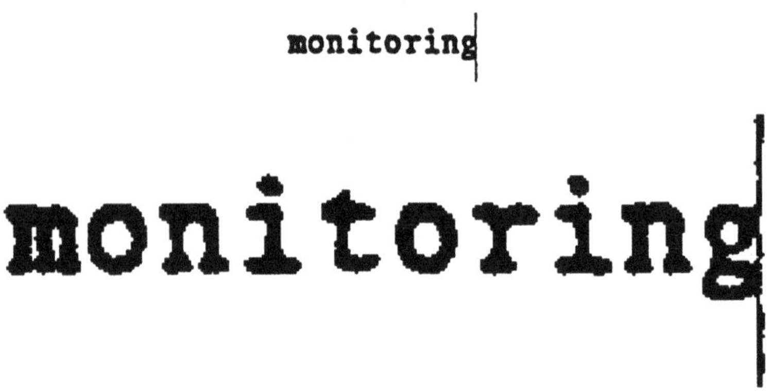

monitoring

monitoring
monitorin
monitorin

5.3 Shaded Backgrounds

In magazines, it is common to find text printed on a shaded background, typically in the form of an inset box or sidebar containing an explanation or digression from the main article. Gray or colored backgrounds are reproduced in printing through the halftoning process. The halftones cause numerous speckles to appear in a bi-level image. The amount of speckling depends on the intensity and color of the shade and on the scanning threshold and resolution. For *01*, *02*, *03*, and *04*, the text shown was printed on a gray background. Device 1 is more troubled by the speckles than the other two systems.

5.3 *01*

Universal Studios

rsalStudios
universal studies
Vniversal Studios

5.3 *02*

Munson presented

<nil>
-Munson presented
Munaon presented

5.3 *03*

National League of Cities,

National League of Cities,

National League of Cities,

National Wage tiff - s,
National Leagoe of ~
National Leagu, of Cities,

5.3 *04*

The order

The order

The order

<nil>
Ine~ ~order
The order

The characters of *05* and *06* were printed on green and beige backgrounds, respectively. Here the color response of the light detectors in the scanner enters into play: some colors are more troublesome than others. Some scanners are entirely blind to red, or to blue, which are used as "dropout" colors on preprinted forms. Many of these problems should be eliminated by gray-scale and color scanning.

If the speckling is severe enough, none of the systems can recognize the text. The gray backgrounds of *07* and *08* provide such examples. The regular speckling is caused by the halftoning process. If an OCR system is given a gray-scale image instead of a bi-level image, then it will have a much better chance of distinguishing the foreground characters from the background noise.

5.3 *07*

Meridian

<nil>

~

<nil>

5.3 *08*

easiLy understand it

<nil>

~

<nil>

5.4 Reverse Video

When light text is printed on a dark background, we get the "reverse video" effect. Such text is called "reverse text" or "inverse text." An OCR system is accustomed to characters composed of black pixels. Thus, if it is able to determine that a region contains reverse text, it will likely invert the region (that is, convert each white pixel to black and each black pixel to white) before attempting to recognize the characters. For this reason, the examples presented in this section show the magnified image in both the original and inverted forms. Device 2 correctly identifies the characters in *01* and *02*. Device 1 is close, but Device 3 does not seem to detect the presence of reverse text.

5.4 *01*

DAILY

DALLY
DAILY
<nil>

5.4
02
New York, NY
New York, NY
New York, NY
New York, NY
New York NIY
New York, NY

Device 2 is able to handle *03* and *04*, but all three systems struggle with *05* and *06*.

5.4 *05*

MANAGING

MANAGING

MANAGING

MANAGING

L
lmlml'lim
<nil>

5.4 *06*

FUND

FUND

FUND

FUND

FDHD
FNNB
I-

Even if an OCR system correctly determines that a region contains reverse text and inverts it, it may have to contend with defects in the inverted image. For example, characters are broken in *07* and *08*. The light orange background in *09* caused small holes in the original image that become speckles when inverted. A blurry green background in *10* created fuzzy characters.

5.4 *07*

FIDELITY

1 11)11.1.1T1-

E’

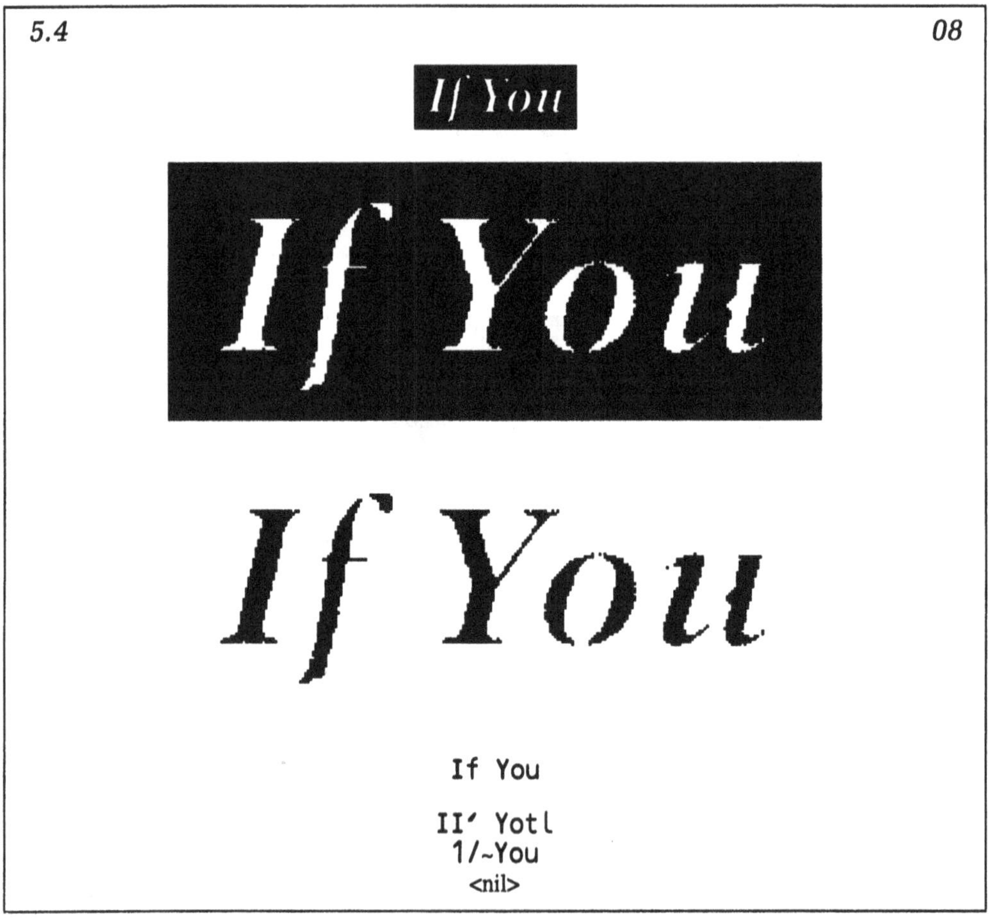
5.4
08
If You
If You
If You
If You
II' Yotl
1/~You
<nil>

5.4
09
RANCHO MIRAGE,
RANCHO MIRAGE,
RANCHO MIRAGE,
RANCHO MIRAGE,
<nil>
RANCHO MIRAGE,

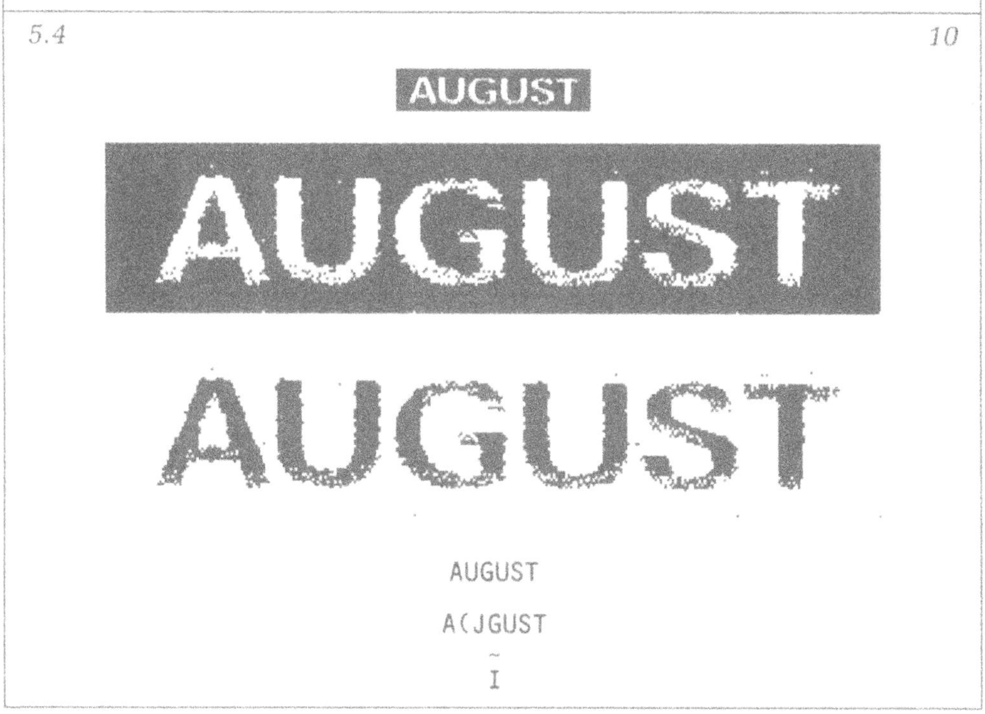
5.4
10
AUGUST
AUGUST
AUGUST
AUGUST
A(JGUST

Sometimes reverse text appears with normal text on the same line. In this case, it is important to invert only the reverse text. If the normal text is also inverted, then reverse text is created, as shown in *11*. Only Device 2 is able to recognize both reverse and normal characters in this example.

5.4 *11*

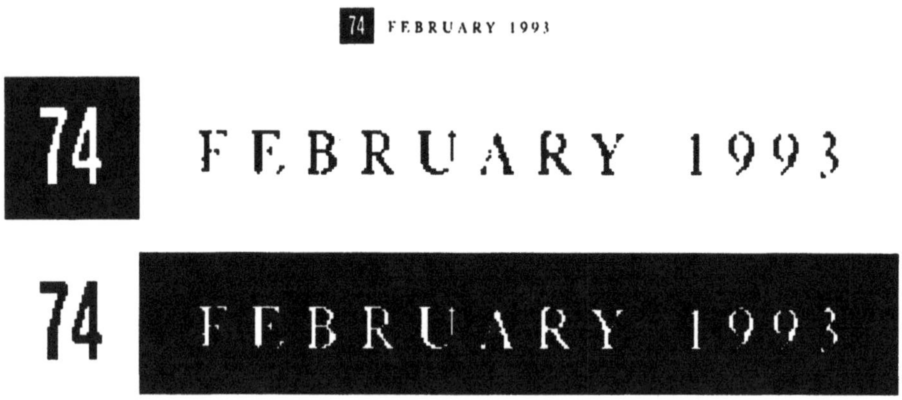

74 FEBRUARY 1993

r BRU.\RY 993
74 FI?BRU.-\RY 199;
I F B R ~ .\ R Y I 993

In *12*, light characters were printed with a dark shadow on a shaded background. When the image is inverted, the text becomes dark with a light shadow, but the speckled background remains speckled. It is not surprising that none of the systems can handle this complexity.

5.4 *12*

IN BRIEF

<nil>

~

<nil>

In *13*, the word an was stylishly printed in beige on a blue background. The beige print was dark enough to create speckles within the letters of the original image, which become holes when the image is inverted. The design of the typeface contributes additional holes, making this a very difficult recognition task (yet trivial for humans).

5.4
13
an
an
an
an
id!
~
<nil>

5.5 Unusual Typefaces

OCR systems are well trained to recognize the characters in common typefaces such as Courier, Helvetica, and Times. Since the characters of Bodoni are not too different from the characters of Times, a system may be able to recognize them without any additional training. However, Madison and Old English are not so standard (see page 114), and the system may be confounded without special training.

The baroque typeface in *01* features an R with a bewildering flourish and r's that resemble z's. The typefaces of *02* and *03* exhibit fancy W's. Notice also the short-legged P and R's in *02*, and the shadow in *03* designed to give the characters a three-dimensional look. Thick, stubby strokes are the style in *04*.

5.5 *01*

```
Reporters

J?epoztez'
cReIbozteu
CRepoziezi
```

5.5 **02**

BRIDGE PARKWAY

BRIDGE PARKWAY

BRIDGE PARKWAY

BPIDGE PARKWAY
<nil>
~RIDGF PARKWAY

5.5 **03**

MOWING

MOWING

MOWING

MOWING
Miow'lns
MoWINg

5.5 **04**

DRINKING

DRINKING

DRINKING

DRIJKIC
DRINKING
PRINKIN~

In most typefaces, the height-to-width aspect ratio of an N is about 1.4:1. Exaggerated aspect ratios are illustrated by the tall, menacing strokes of *05* and *06*, and the squat, stubborn capitals in *07*. Contrast the lowercase o's in *06* with the uppercase O in *07*. The U in *07* is so wide that two systems split it into LJ, and Device 2 divides the H into I-I.

5.5 *05*

What

What

What

Whal
WLiaL
What

5.5 *06*

A Lot to Do

A Lot to Do

A Lot to Do

A Lot to Do
Ll teL le Lie
A Lot 1000

5.5 *07*

SOUTH

SOUTH

SOUTH

SOUTH
SGLJTI-I
S~LJYH

The elegant 4's are a problem in *08*. "Old style" numerals are shown in *09*: the 5 and 7 dip below the baseline, and the 1 resembles an I. We will see more unusual typefaces in the next section.

5.5 *08*

Page A4, Column 4

Page A4, Column 4

```
Page A4, Column 4

Page Ad, Column 4
Page At, Column 1;
Pooe A4, Column 1'
```

5.5 *09*

T. 15 S., R. 70 E.

T. 15 S., R. 70 E.

```
T. 15 S., R. 70 E.

T. is s., R. 70 E.
T. IS S., R. 70 E.
T. `5 S., R. 70 E.
```

5.6 Very Large Print

Very large print is not intrinsically difficult to recognize. However, OCR systems are optimized for the normal-size print that comprises the bulk of their diet. To contend with very large characters, a system may "normalize" them, that is, reduce them to the size of 10-point or 12-point characters, before attempting to identify them. However, this process can distort their shape because *display type* is designed to be viewed at a large size.

In this section, we present examples of very large print. They are shown only in actual size, without the 4X enlargement used elsewhere. To gain an idea of how large they really are, imagine an entire paragraph set in the illustrated size.

To increase the legibility of large type, relatively tight letterspacing is commonly used, which can make it difficult for OCR systems to isolate individual characters. In *01*, we see large characters that are kerned and touching. Only one system identifies the kerned `fa` in *02*, but all three can handle the kerned `fe` in *03*. The oversized apostrophe in *03* is another matter.

5.6 *01*

Africa

`Africa`

`Afnea`
`Africa`
`Mrica`

5.6 *02*

face

face

1 ace
<nil>
face

5.6 *03*

feds'

feds'

feds,
fedse
feds'

Bold characters are placed very close together in *04*, *05*, and *06*. Contrast their thick, crowded strokes with the delicate, widely-spaced characters in *07*. The characters in *05* are afflicted with tiny holes. The characters in *06* are surrounded by speckles from a beige background.

5.6 *04*

ravaged

ravaged

roveged
ruvugecl
ravaged

5.6 *05*

SLAIN

SLAIN

SLlIN

~
L IN

5.6 *06*

RACE

RACE

<nil>
RAGE
Rq

5.6 *07*

Cladding

Cladding

C:tadcting
Claddmg
C1&ddin~

Device 2 is baffled by the tall, narrow characters in *08*, *09*, and *10*. The height-to-width aspect ratio of the **N** in *08* is 2:1.

5.6 *08*

GOINGS

GOINGS

GoLNGS
toLues
GOIHGS

5.6 *09*

TV TIMES

TV TIMES

TU TIMES
<nil>
IV IIMCS

5.6 *10*

DIPLOMACY

DIPLOMACY

DLPLOMIC!
<nil>
DIPLOMACY

An unusual typeface is shown in *11*. Aside from the spiraling flourishes (known as *swashes*), the horizontal strokes are very thin compared to the vertical strokes. Device 3 seems to ignore the horizontal strokes, generating `i)` for `P` and `ji` for `p`. Notice also how the two `e`'s differ in appearance. In *12*, Device 2 ably separates the kerned italic characters, but breaks the `n` in the process.

5.6 *11*

People

People

People,
6Pe ople;
i)c 0jil~

5.6 *12*

Experiences

Experiences

Expenences
Experiertces
~cn~ences

The mammoth 5 in *13*, the Ag conglomerate in *14*, and the four inseparable giants in *15* appear too large to be accepted as bona fide characters by Devices 2 and 3. The characters of *15* were printed in purple with a pale orange shadow and exemplify some of the biggest tests that lie in wait for OCR systems.

5.6 *13*

5

5

5
<nil>
<nil>

5.6 *14*

Age

Age

Age
<nil>
<nil>

5.6 *15*

TEST

TEST

<nil>

~

<nil>

5.7 Very Small Print

Humans struggle to read very small print so it is not surprising that computers struggle also. Minute smudges of ink or toner have a more damaging effect on small characters than large characters. Important details of small characters may be lost when scanning at 300 dpi, and a higher resolution may be beneficial. Although OCR systems are optimized for normal-size print, they should not neglect small characters ("Read the fine print!").

Small, muddy characters are shown in *01*, *02*, *03*, and *04*. Gaps between characters, and openings within characters, are closed. Remarkably, Device 2 misses only two characters in *01* and correctly identifies the second word in *02*. The d, e, and a's in *03* are completely filled, and only the tiniest opening remains inside the o; however, the systems recognize the d from its silhouette. A lightly-shaded background contributed some of the noise in *04*.

5.7 *01*

Settlingstones Mines

Settlingstones Mines

```
Settlingstones Mines

Settlin6etone. Mln e
Settlingstcnem Mines
Settlinguton.. Nines
```

5.7 *02*

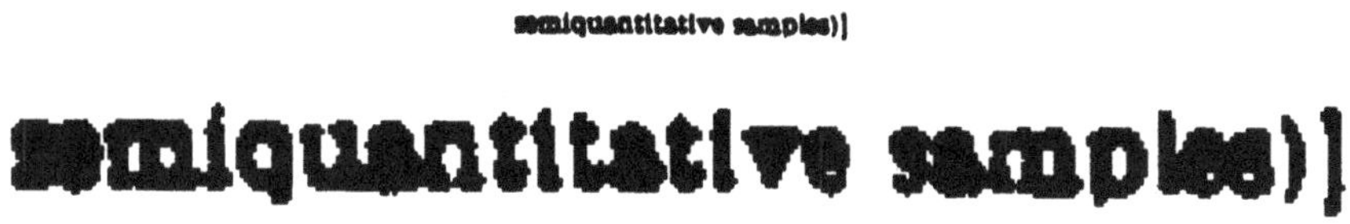

semiquantitative samples)]

armlq structure uncles)
mmlquantltatlvs samples)}
mmlqtsntltatl'a 'amplull

5.7 *03*

Gatorade

Bade
hterede
~srsd.

5.7 *04*

BLADE RUNNER

81,681! WINNER
BLAOE IIIIIINEII
BLADE IIUNNER

It is no simple task to separate the letters of Conshohocken in *05*. A postal address reader, with its knowledge of city-state-zip combinations, might be able to decode it. The three systems fare much better with the isolated capitals in *06*. The narrow italics in *07* are widely spaced but badly deformed.

5.7 *05*

Conshohocken, PA 19428

Conshohocken, PA 19428

Conshohocken, PA 19428

Men, PA 19428
Conmohodxm PA 19428
COrwohod(~PA 194w

5.7 *06*

EDUCATION STATISTICS, 1991;

EDUCATION STATISTICS, 1991;

EDUCATION STATISTICS, 1991;

EDUCATION9TATIaTIC8,1991:
EDUCATION STATISTICS, lggl;
EOUCATION STATISTICS. 1551.

5.7 *07*

Workstation

Workstation

Workstation

Worlstarzon
Wurkirannn
~`0 rks to tOn

In *08* and *09*, small characters are printed lightly and break where they are thinnest: horizontal strokes and NE-SW diagonals. Pieces are missing from a few characters in *10* and *11*. The wide inter-character spacing in *07* and *11* induces Device 3 to generate space characters.

5.7 *08*

VEGETABLE KABOBS

VEGETABLE KABOBS

VEGETABLE KABOBS

VEGET.\BI.E K.\BOBS
VEGETr\BIiI`l KABOBS
vFGF.TABLE KABOBS

5.7 *09*

ASSOCIATED PRESS

ASSOCIATED PRESS

ASSOCIATED PRESS

ASSOCIA'I'ED l'ltESS
Asstieimun mass
A~otIATF.O i'HE5~

5.7 *10*

REHABILITATION CENTER

REHABILITATION CENTER

REHABILITATION CENTER

RFHAS I TATION CENTER
REHABMTATTON CENTER
RE~AE TACOR CERTAR

5.7 *11*

CORPORATION

CORPORA riON
COHPORAHON
CO k HO RA IC N

Very small digits are shown in *12*, *13*, and *14*. Surprisingly, both 4's in *12* were correctly identified, presumably from their silhouette. An OCR system might consider a mixed sequence of tiny letters and digits, such as those in *13* and *14*, to be aggravated harassment. Determining the case (upper or lower) of the SC in *13* and the VC in *14* is very difficult. In *15*, the systems try to determine the case of VERY SMALL CAPS.

5.7 *12*

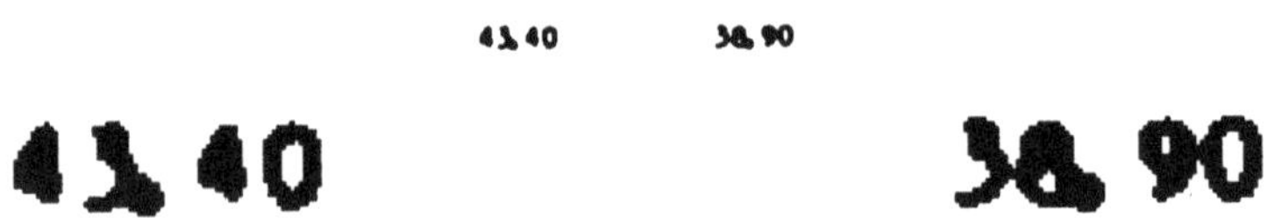

43.40 38.90

43.40 be so
4140 90.00
4-4G 3&90

5.7 *13*

0217-0031SC

0217-0031SC

0217-0031SC

SO.
@21l=@0$1$C
021?.003iSC

5.7 *14*

VC722A 12/14/93

VC722A 12/14/93

VC722A 12/14/93

VC722A 2/14/93
vc722A i2/MI93
vC722A 12/1A193

5.7 *15*

RAYBURN HOUSE

RAYBURN HOUSE

RAYBURN HOUSE

RAYBURN HOUSE
RAYBURN House
RAYBURN HOuSE

Chapter 6

Conclusion

"When you come to a fork in the road, take it."

— Yogi Berra

A seven-year-old child can identify characters with far greater accuracy than the leading OCR systems. Through many examples, we have seen the variety of problems at the OCR frontier. No single technique can solve all of these problems; however, there are many ways to advance the state of the art. We discuss four approaches:

1. Improved image processing.

2. Adapting to the current document.

3. Multi-character recognition.

4. Increased use of linguistic context.

Improved image processing aims to alleviate the effects of imaging flaws like stray marks and curved baselines, as well as certain typographical features like underlining, shaded backgrounds, and reverse video. Some of the necessary techniques have already been developed, but are still too resource-intensive for the current generation of desktop computers. Filtering algorithms process a 3×3 or 5×5 window centered on every single pixel of the image; detecting large interfering marks requires even more processing. Algorithms for straightening curved baselines are equally time-consuming.

Increased computational resources enable high-resolution gray-scale and color images to be analyzed. A gray-scale image can be converted to a bi-level image while adjusting for uneven contrast using a technique known as *adaptive local binarization*. By recognizing characters directly from a gray-scale image, fine or faint strokes are more easily detected. High-resolution images reduce the edge effects that are the primary source of noise in very small print. Color scanning will eliminate problems due to colored print and shaded backgrounds.

There have been attempts to model mathematically the types of noise found in page images, in the hope that such models will allow the automatic generation of immense data sets for training OCR systems. This approach may lead to systems that are less sensitive to point-spread distortion and other types of imaging noise.

Adapting to the current document means exploiting the consistency of the document's typography. Although there are egregious exceptions like ransom notes and typeface catalogs, a single font is used throughout most documents. Systems that recognize only the characters of a single font are faster and far more accurate than *omnifont* systems which attempt to identify characters from all fonts at once. There is good reason for this: type designers are careful to maintain distinctions between symbols within the same typeface. An omnifont system may confuse a character from one font with a similar-looking, but different character from another font.

Early OCR systems could recognize only a single font. A trainable OCR system can learn to recognize new fonts, but only with considerable effort on the part of the user. These difficulties, combined with the need to recognize multi-font documents, have spawned today's omnifont systems. However, looking for characters from all fonts within a single document has its disadvantages. Although such a system is prepared for the worst, it is not streamlined for homogeneous documents. When a system is tuned to the current font, accuracy and speed are enhanced.

Most OCR systems ignore a rich source of training data. After a human editor corrects errors in OCR output, an OCR system can use this feedback to optimize its performance on similar documents.

Multi-character recognition avoids the error-prone process of character segmentation by recognizing a group of characters as a unit. One option is to recognize entire words, under the assumption that inter-word blanks can be readily detected. The silhouette or outline of a word shows the relative location of ascenders, descenders, and capitals. (Comparing silhouettes would prevent Cables from being considered for pebbles in *2.2-27*.) Among words with the same outline, identifying just one or two letters is often enough to disambiguate them. However, this technique does not work for numbers or words in all-caps.

Multi-character recognition can be accomplished systematically by processing the pixels that appear in a moving window of several character-widths. The mathematical foundations (*Hidden Markov Models*) have already been developed for cursive handwriting recognition and speech recognition, and the resulting algorithms are now beginning to be applied to machine-printed text. The most ambitious of these algorithms attempts to recognize an entire page as a single unit.

Increased use of linguistic context, beyond the use of a lexicon, contributes further to resolving ambiguities. Many OCR systems will choose a common character sequence like ing over a rare one like lng based on *n-gram* statistics, which specify the relative frequency of two-character sequences (*bi-grams*) and three-character sequences (*tri-grams*) for the language of the document. It is also helpful to know whether a sequence is a common prefix or suffix.

The use of word frequencies is beneficial. A few hundred common words (like the, and, of, to) account for more than half of the words appearing in normal English text. The word are is much more likely to appear than the word arc. These frequencies can be adjusted to reflect expected document composition; for example, war appears more often than wax in documents at the Pentagon, but much less often at a candle factory (*3.2-14*). Special terms that appear frequently should be added to the lexicon, including names (Holt, *2.1-04*; Haley, *2.2-14*), technical terms (permeabilities, *2.1-25*; Pinus longaeva, *5.1-04*), and abbreviations (ANSI, *3.1-04*; keV, *3.2-21*).

OCR systems can benefit also from syntax analysis. The phrase, `leek tar fail, tar lent` (*2.1-26*), is clearly ungrammatical. Semantic analysis could enable an OCR system to avoid meaningless yet grammatically-correct phrases like `wages of lake level` (*2.2-01*). Of course, the effectiveness of using linguistic context is limited by the possibility that the page contains unexpected constructs, including nonsense words, ungrammatical phrases, and sentences that defy semantic interpretation. A novel typically contains fewer irregular constructs than technical material (especially books about OCR).

The techniques mentioned in this chapter are by no means exhaustive or mutually exclusive. Not only can they be combined with other methods within a single OCR system, but several OCR systems based on entirely different principles can be combined. In such a scheme, the systems vote for the identity of characters. Since different systems seldom make the same mistake, this democratic process reduces the error rate.

On the basis of the diversity of errors that we have encountered, we believe that further progress will result from combinations of techniques and not from the discovery of any single overarching principle.

Our survey of the OCR frontier is not exhaustive: there are other sources of OCR error not covered by our examples. Typographic puzzles include majuscules, ligatures, and *script* typefaces. Low-resolution page images (such as fax images) and dot-matrix print give OCR systems a coarser view than the 300 dpi images we have examined.

A line of text is expected to be horizontal; its deviation from horizontal is called its *skew angle*. Recognition accuracy suffers greatly when this angle exceeds two degrees. Skew is caused by photocopying or scanning a page that is positioned obliquely on the platen (a fairly common occurrence when using an automatic document feeder). Before attempting to recognize characters, an OCR system may check the page image for skew and apply corrective measures. Skew detection and skew correction algorithms have been incorporated into many of today's OCR systems; however, we did not evaluate these algorithms.

An OCR system must first locate the text within a page image before it can identify the characters. The user may provide the location of the text regions (called *zones*) through a process known as *manual zoning*, or the system may perform *automatic zoning* to find the text without user assistance. In successful automatic zoning, the system locates all of the text on the page while excluding non-text objects such as photographs and line drawings. Furthermore, the system determines the reading order of the text regions so that it can write its output in the correct sequence. For example, the text generated for the left-hand column of a two-column page should precede the text produced for the right-hand column. Nearly all of today's OCR systems provide automatic zoning as an option. Evaluating this feature is outside the scope of this book, yet choices made by an automatic zoning algorithm can affect the character recognition process.

Although this book is English-centric, many OCR systems that process English can also process a number of other Western European languages. These systems possess a lexicon for each of these languages and can recognize their accented letters and unique punctuation. A greater challenge is posed by non-Roman scripts, such as Russian, Arabic, and Chinese; however, OCR systems have been designed to process these languages. Few OCR systems automatically determine the language of a document, so the user must provide this information. Most systems are unprepared for pages containing more than one language.

Although we have focused on machine-printed text, the field of OCR also encompasses the recognition of "human-printed" text, that is, hand print and cursive writing. An OCR system for handwritten text is an *online* system if it detects and utilizes the pen movements of the writer to improve its accuracy; online systems provide a primary interface to many hand-held computing devices. *Offline* systems lack this stroke information and are used to read handwritten form entries, bank check amounts, and postal addresses. Consider how much more difficult OCR becomes without the consistency and clarity of machine print.

As OCR technology improves, it becomes suitable for and is deployed in more and more applications. The use of OCR systems has grown tremendously over the past 40 years due to significant advances in the field and the ever-increasing computing power available for the task. We expect this trend to continue, and although OCR systems may never match human performance, the gap will narrow.

In conclusion, we have immensely enjoyed this exploration of the OCR frontier, and we hope that we have left behind ample guideposts. There is much more territory to explore, and we look forward to further surveys.

Further Reading

A history of the field of Optical Character Recognition has been compiled by a former executive of Recognition International, a prominent OCR manufacturer. The emphasis of this volume is OCR applications, from 19th-century patents for readers for the blind, through invoice processing in the 1950s, to high-speed readers of forms and cash-register tapes in the late 1970s.

Herbert F. Schantz.
The History of OCR.
Recognition Technologies Users Association, Boston, 1982.

Work in the OCR field prior to 1964 can be traced through an 800-entry bibliography from IBM. By the late 1970s, so many articles on OCR had been published that the preparation of a comprehensive bibliography became a Herculean task. Nevertheless, there have been two recent efforts to track the field. The Jenkins-Kanai bibliography has over 1100 entries, while the Sabourin bibliography has more than 3700.

F. J. Thomas and L. P. Horwitz.
Character recognition bibliography and classification.
IBM Research Report RC-1088, T. J. Watson Research Center, Yorktown Heights, New York, 1964.

Frank Jenkins and Junichi Kanai.
A keyword-indexed bibliography of character recognition and document analysis (Revision 2.0).
Information Science Research Institute TR-93-07, University of Nevada, Las Vegas, 1993.

Conrad F. Sabourin.
Optical character recognition and document segmentation: Bibliography.
Infolingua Inc., Montreal, 1994.

Perceptual and cognitive aspects of reading and writing are addressed in a bibliography that appeared in a journal devoted to typography.

R. Shillman, C. Cox, T. Kuklinsky, J. Ventura, M. Eden, and B. Blesser.
A bibliography in character recognition techniques for describing characters.
Visible Language 7:151-166, Cleveland, 1974.

The best early summaries of OCR technology, with accurate explanations and still-fresh insights, are Mary Stevens' NBS report, and a small book published by the British Computer Society.

Mary E. Stevens.
Automatic character recognition: State-of-the-art report.
National Bureau of Standards, Technical Note 112, Washington, DC, 1961.

British Computer Society, London.
Character Recognition, 1967.

At least one outstanding text on pattern recognition with a focus on character recognition appears every decade. The authors of the following four books led groups that developed OCR systems in the Soviet Union, the United Kingdom, France, and Germany.

V. A. Kovalevsky, editor.
Character Readers and Pattern Recognition.
Spartan Books, New York, 1968.

Julian Ullmann.
Pattern Recognition Techniques.
Crane, Russak, and Company, New York, 1973.

Morton Nadler and Eric P. Smith.
Pattern Recognition Engineering.
Wiley, New York, 1993.

Jürgen Schürmann.
Pattern Classification.
Wiley, New York, 1996.

The Established Text on statistical pattern recognition has no explicit material on character recognition, but its influence on OCR cannot be overestimated. A new two-volume edition is in the works. This book is not for the mathematically challenged.

Richard Duda and Peter Hart.
Pattern Classification and Scene Analysis.
Wiley, New York, 1973.

We cite two classical papers on OCR: the first lays the theoretical foundations of statistical classification, while the second addresses feature extraction. Thousands of researchers have followed in the footsteps of Chow, Bledsoe, and Browning.

C. K. Chow.
An optimum character recognition system using decision functions.
Transactions on Electronic Computers 6:247-254, Institute of Radio Engineers, New York, 1957.

W. W. Bledsoe and I. Browning.
Pattern recognition and reading by machine.
Proceedings of the Eastern Joint Conference on Computers, pages 225-233, IRE-AIEE-AIChE, New York, 1959.

The 1960s saw a number of conferences devoted primarily to character recognition. Papers from the two conferences below are still cited. The volume edited by Kanal contains perspectives by prominent contributors, including Jacob Rabinow and Israel Sheinberg.

G. L. Fisher, editor.
Optical Character Recognition.
Spartan Books, Washington, DC, 1960.

Laveen N. Kanal, editor.
Pattern Recognition.
Thompson Book Company, Washington, DC, 1968.

After a lull in the 1970s and 1980s, conferences on document image analysis, including character recognition, took a new lease on life. The best papers from several recent conferences can be found in carefully edited volumes by well-known OCR researchers.

Henry S. Baird, Horst Bunke, and Kazuhiko Yamamoto, editors.
Structured Document Image Analysis.
Springer-Verlag, Berlin, 1992.

Horst Bunke, editor.
Advances in Structural and Syntactic Pattern Recognition.
World Scientific, Singapore, 1992.

A. Lawrence Spitz and Andreas Dengel, editors.
Document Analysis Systems.
World Scientific, Singapore, 1995.

Jonathan J. Hull and Suzanne Taylor, editors.
Document Analysis Systems II.
World Scientific, Singapore, 1998.

Technical journals sometimes schedule special issues on character recognition and related subjects. For the following special issues, guest editors invited leading researchers to contribute tutorial and survey articles with comprehensive bibliographies, as well as shorter research reports.

Theodosios Pavlidis and Shunji Mori, editors.
Proceedings of the IEEE 80(7), Special 80th Anniversary Issue on Optical Character Recognition.
IEEE, New York, 1992.

Lawrence O'Gorman and Rangachar Kasturi, editors.
Machine Vision and Applications 5(3), Special Issue on Document Image Analysis Techniques.
Springer International, 1992.

Lawrence O'Gorman and Rangachar Kasturi, editors.
IEEE Computer 25(7), Special Issue on Document Image Analysis Systems.
IEEE Computer Society, Los Alamitos, California, 1992.

In 1995, O'Gorman and Kasturi published an anthology of selected "best" papers on document image analysis, with a tutorial introduction to each topic and an extensive bibliography. This collection includes several papers from the aforementioned special issues.

Lawrence O'Gorman and Rangachar Kasturi, editors.
Document Image Analysis.
IEEE Computer Society Press, Los Alamitos, California, 1995.

The next two books address a wealth of subjects related to OCR, including text and image compression, document preparation systems, digital typesetting, and digital halftoning. They also cover document interchange formats such as Office Document Architecture (ODA) and Standard Generalized Markup Language (SGML).

Hsieh S. Hou.
Digital Document Processing.
Wiley, New York, 1983.

J. C. Van Vliet, editor.
Document Manipulation and Typography.
Cambridge University Press, 1988.

For the reader interested in an authoritative treatment of typography, we recommend the lavishly illustrated volume by McLean.

Ruari McLean.
Thames and Hudson Manual of Typography.
Thames and Hudson, London, 1980.

Many aspects of the use of linguistic context are explored in an anthology compiled by Srihari.

Sargur N. Srihari, editor.
Computer Text Recognition and Error Correction.
IEEE Computer Society Press, Los Alamitos, California, 1985.

An article by Nagy and Seth introduces OCR to readers from other disciplines.

George Nagy and Sharad Seth.
Modern optical character recognition.
The Froehlich/Kent Encyclopedia of Telecommunications, Volume 11, pages 473-531, Marcel Dekker, New York, 1996.

Conference proceedings provide the bulk of current information on character recognition techniques. The largest pattern recognition meeting is the biennial International Conference on Pattern Recognition (ICPR), started in 1973. Since 1991, the major forum for document analysis research has been the biennial International Conference on Document Analysis and Recognition (ICDAR).

From 1992 through 1996, the Information Science Research Institute (ISRI) at the University of Nevada, Las Vegas, hosted the Symposium on Document Analysis and Information Retrieval (SDAIR), which attracted OCR and Information Retrieval users, researchers, and product developers. At this forum, ISRI presented the results of its annual test of the leading OCR systems. These results can be found in the following technical reports.

Stephen V. Rice, Junichi Kanai, and Thomas A. Nartker.
A report on the accuracy of OCR devices.
ISRI TR-92-02, University of Nevada, Las Vegas, 1992.

Stephen V. Rice, Junichi Kanai, and Thomas A. Nartker.
An evaluation of OCR accuracy.
ISRI TR-93-01, University of Nevada, Las Vegas, 1993.

Stephen V. Rice, Junichi Kanai, and Thomas A. Nartker.
The third annual test of OCR accuracy.
ISRI TR-94-03, University of Nevada, Las Vegas, 1994.

Stephen V. Rice, Frank R. Jenkins, and Thomas A. Nartker.
The fourth annual test of OCR accuracy.
ISRI TR-95-04, University of Nevada, Las Vegas, 1995.

Stephen V. Rice, Frank R. Jenkins, and Thomas A. Nartker.
The fifth annual test of OCR accuracy.
ISRI TR-96-01, University of Nevada, Las Vegas, 1996.

OCR test data, including document page images and corresponding "ground-truth" text, and computer software for OCR testing, are available from ISRI. For more information, write: Information Science Research Institute, University of Nevada, Las Vegas, 4505 Maryland Parkway, Box 454021, Las Vegas, Nevada 89154-4021, USA.

Appendix
Source of Examples

Id	Page	Text	Source
2.1-01	10	Mission	U.S. Department of Energy technical report (table)
2.1-02	11	Man-Made	U.S. Department of Energy technical report (table)
2.1-03	11	Unnamed Mineral	Los Alamos Scientific Laboratory technical report (table)
2.1-04	12	Holt (1984).	U.S. Department of Energy technical report
2.1-05	12	1984	Lawrence Berkeley Laboratory technical report (footnote)
2.1-06	13	section 102(2)(C)	Nuclear Waste Policy Act of 1982
2.1-07	14	MECHANICAL	Bechtel presentation slide (figure caption)
2.1-08	14	RECOMMENDATIONS	U.S. Nuclear Regulatory Commission technical report
2.1-09	15	See HISTORY,	*Washington Post* newspaper article
2.1-10	15	CONTENTS	U.S. Department of Energy technical report
2.1-11	16	LAS VEGAS,	letter from the Clark County, Nevada, School District (letterhead)
2.1-12	16	Lap-top	*Endless Vacation* magazine article
2.1-13	17	(sage)	U.S. Geological Survey technical report
2.1-14	17	Nonhydrocarbons	Rocky Mountain Association of Geologists technical report (table)

Id	Page	Text	Source
2.1-15	18	sites	U.S. Nuclear Regulatory Commission public hearing transcript
2.1-16	18	Compositions	U.S. Department of Energy technical report (table)
2.1-17	19	differences	U.S. Department of Energy technical report (figure caption)
2.1-18	19	weight loss	*Weight Watchers Magazine* article (photo caption)
2.1-19	19	Fractional deviation	Westinghouse Electric technical report (figure caption)
2.1-20	20	Western	U.S. Geological Survey technical report
2.1-21	20	McGovern	*Golf Magazine* article
2.1-22	20	From Journal	*Milwaukee Journal* newspaper article
2.1-23	21	long-term	Battelle Pacific Northwest Laboratory technical report
2.1-24	21	Waste Form	U.S. Department of Energy technical report
2.1-25	21	permeabilities	International Atomic Energy Agency technical report
2.1-26	22	look for fall, far left:	*McCall's* magazine article (photo caption)
2.1-27	22	simplified	*PC Magazine* article (photo caption)
2.1-28	23	functions.	*Popular Mechanics* magazine article (photo caption)
2.1-29	23	Minister Andrei	*Tampa Tribune* newspaper article
2.1-30	23	values in silver	FMC Corporation technical report
2.1-31	24	Diagrammatic	Nevada Water Resources Bulletin technical report (figure caption)
2.1-32	25	Number	U.S. Department of Energy technical report (table)
2.1-33	25	of some magnitude.	*Chicago Tribune Magazine* article

Id	Page	Text	Source
2.1-34	26	Washington Post Staff Writers	*Washington Post* newspaper article
2.1-35	26	time-stratigraphy:	Nevada Bureau of Mines technical report
2.2-01	27	Changes of lake level	U.S. Geological Survey technical report
2.2-02	27	A step size	*Geomechanics Abstracts* journal article (figure caption)
2.2-03	28	Fig. 16, p. 36	U.S. Department of Energy technical report
2.2-04	28	it crushed earthen	*St. Louis Post-Dispatch* newspaper article
2.2-05	29	Alameda, CA 94501-1095	letter from Ingres (letterhead)
2.2-06	29	Imaging Experts	letter from Media Cybernetics (letterhead)
2.2-07	30	A Not-For Profit Organization	letter from NAEIR (letterhead)
2.2-08	30	General Manager	letter from the Olive Garden Restaurant (letterhead)
2.2-09	31	Saltbush.	*Proceedings of the American Society of Civil Engineers* journal article
2.2-10	31	OIL SHALE	Nevada Bureau of Mines technical report
2.2-11	32	SOUTH CENTRAL	U.S. Geological Survey technical report (page header)
2.2-12	32	VOLCANIC	U.S. Geological Survey technical report (page header)
2.2-13	32	TIMBER MOUNTAIN	U.S. Geological Survey technical report (page header)
2.2-14	33	Haley (1960).	U.S. Geological Survey technical report (table)
2.2-15	33	Howard R.Hughes	letter from an individual
2.2-16	34	Life	*Boston Globe* newspaper article
2.2-17	34	Las Vegas	letter from Prince of Peace Catholic Church

Id	Page	Text	Source
2.2-18	35	8500-mile	*Car and Driver* magazine article
2.2-19	35	L. D. Gordon	Nevada Bureau of Mines technical report
2.2-20	36	route to Tonopah	Nevada Bureau of Mines technical report
2.2-21	36	plots should be read	*Water Resources Research* journal article
2.2-22	37	as a function	Florida State University technical report (figure caption)
2.2-23	37	Scholtz	Los Alamos Scientific Laboratory technical report
2.2-24	38	decomposition	supplement to the book, *Inorganic and Theoretical Chemistry*
2.2-25	38	desuperposition	*Society of Petroleum Engineers Journal* article
2.2-26	39	claylike	U.S. Geological Survey technical report
2.2-27	39	pebbles	Nevada Bureau of Mines technical report
2.2-28	40	Garth Brooks	*People* magazine article (photo caption)
2.2-29	40	southern Maryland	*Journal of Geophysical Research* article (figure caption)
2.2-30	41	direct-dialed,	letter from AT&T (footnote)
2.2-31	42	The work involved	Energy Research and Development Administration technical report
2.2-32	42	available at Payless	*'Teen* magazine article
2.2-33	42	State University	letter from Penn State (letterhead)
2.2-34	43	Registered	letter from Princor Financial Services (letterhead)
2.2-35	43	High Level	Lawrence Livermore National Laboratory technical report
2.3-01	44	seismograph	University of Wisconsin-Milwaukee technical report
2.3-02	44	test results	Nippon Steel technical report (figure caption)

Id	Page	Text	Source
2.3-03	45	United States	letter from the U.S. Department of Agriculture (letterhead)
2.3-04	45	THE PRINTED WORD,	*People* magazine article
2.3-05	45	LAKE BONNEVILLE	U.S. Geological Survey monograph
2.3-06	46	private gifts supporting	letter from the University of Illinois Foundation (letterhead)
2.3-07	46	Northwestern University	letter from Americans United for Life (letterhead)
2.3-08	46	Office of Membership	letter from the Association for Computing Machinery (letterhead)
2.4-01	47	Great Lakes	the book, *The Last Great Ice Sheets* (figure caption)
2.4-02	47	tanks	*Cleveland Plain Dealer* newspaper article
2.4-03	48	easy to live with.	*St. Petersburg Times* newspaper article
2.4-04	48	Young	*Dallas Morning News* article
2.4-05	49	found	*Buffalo News* article
2.4-06	49	was found	University of Nevada, Reno, Master's thesis
2.4-07	50	Nye County	Nevada Bureau of Mines technical report (page header)
2.4-08	50	and verse	*Los Angeles Times* newspaper article
2.4-09	51	It can be seen	Sandia National Laboratories technical report
2.4-10	52	have	*St. Petersburg Times* newspaper article
2.4-11	52	cholesterol	*Ladies' Home Journal* magazine article
2.4-12	53	both."	*Sports Illustrated* magazine article
2.4-13	53	will	*Philadelphia Inquirer* newspaper article
2.4-14	54	period of the	U.S. Geological Survey monograph
2.4-15	54	Sincerely,	letter from Navy Engineering Programs
2.4-16	55	subscription	letter from *Health After 50* magazine

Id	Page	Text	Source
2.4-17	55	See CLINTON/8A	newspaper article
2.5-01	58	time of their	*Bulletin of the Geological Society of America* journal article
2.5-02	58	van Olphen	*American Mineralogist* journal article
2.5-03	59	extend his appreciation	*Bulletin of the Geological Society of America* journal article
2.5-04	59	Twelve wells	U.S. Geological Survey technical report (table)
2.5-05	60	movement	University of California, Berkeley, Ph.D. dissertation
2.5-06	60	before publication	U.S. *Federal Register*
3.1-01	62	1968	U.S. Geological Survey technical report (figure caption)
3.1-02	63	He was 81.	*Minneapolis Star Tribune* newspaper article
3.1-03	63	White-Inyo	University of California, Berkeley, Ph.D. dissertation
3.1-04	64	ANSI/ASME	American Society of Mechanical Engineers technical report (page header)
3.1-05	64	1/4-lb.	*Country Woman* magazine article
3.1-06	65	Fig. 1b.	Chalmers University of Technology technical report
3.1-07	65	Proc. 1st Cong.	the book, *Introduction to Rock Mechanics*
3.1-08	65	I-57: Left lane	*Chicago Sun-Times* newspaper article
3.1-09	66	1 percent level	U.S. Geological Survey technical report
3.1-10	66	less than 1 meter	the book, *Economic Mineral Deposits*
3.1-11	67	I have learned	letter from Ameriprint
3.1-12	67	Langmuir, I.	the book, *Introduction to Soil Physics*
3.1-13	68	11 grams;	*Country Living* magazine article (footnote)
3.1-14	68	Ghostbusters II	*Playboy* magazine article

Id	Page	Text	Source
3.1-15	69	19th-century	*Victoria* magazine article (photo caption)
3.1-16	69	[6]	American Nuclear Society technical report
3.1-17	70	up to 60 m/s,	U.S. Geological Survey technical report
3.1-18	70	1.2 million	*Newark Star-Ledger* newspaper article (headline)
3.1-19	71	Penrose, R. A. F., Jr.	Nevada Bureau of Mines technical report
3.1-20	71	San Jacinto	the book, *Natural Regions of the United States and Canada*
3.1-21	72	Dr. Albrecht Heim,	U.S. Geological Survey monograph (footnote)
3.1-22	72	my husband, Allen,	*Country* magazine article
3.2-01	74	PO Box 10864	Sandia National Laboratories technical report
3.2-02	74	89101	letter from Palm Memorial Estate Plans (letterhead)
3.2-03	75	1000s	U.S. Department of Energy technical report (table)
3.2-04	75	10CFR960	U.S. Geological Survey technical report
3.2-05	76	Quaternary	U.S. Geological Survey technical report
3.2-06	76	APPENDIX D	Los Alamos Scientific Laboratory technical report
3.2-07	77	$1,000-a-day	*Working Woman* magazine article
3.2-08	77	02:49:41.0	U.S. Geological Survey technical report (table)
3.2-09	78	Nonmedical	*Consumers Digest* magazine article
3.2-10	78	quantative	U.S. Department of Energy public hearing transcript
3.2-11	79	in G-Tunnel	U.S. Department of Energy technical report
3.2-12	79	GARRELS	*Geochimica et Cosmochimica Acta* journal article

Id	Page	Text	Source
3.2-13	79	FIGURE 26	U.S. Geological Survey technical report (figure caption)
3.2-14	80	Wax plug	U.S. Geological Survey technical report (photo caption)
3.2-15	80	J. Bonk	Sandia National Laboratories technical report
3.2-16	81	discontinua	U.S. Nuclear Regulatory Commission regulatory guide
3.2-17	81	glass-enclosed aeries	*Philadelphia Inquirer* newspaper article
3.2-18	82	We've	letter from American Express
3.2-19	82	THE MAPLE PRESS	the book, *Ore Deposits of the United States, 1933-1967*
3.2-20	83	BookStore.	letter from the Association for Information and Image Management
3.2-21	83	74.67 keV	Lawrence Berkeley Laboratory technical report
3.2-22	84	FIGURE B.5.	Sandia National Laboratories technical report (figure caption)
3.2-23	84	B03, B17, B41,	Hanford Engineering Development Laboratory technical report (table)
3.2-24	85	37891S	U.S. Department of Energy technical report
3.2-25	85	well 5C	U.S. Geological Survey technical report
4.1-01	89	In consequence, the	International Commission on Radiological Protection technical report
4.1-02	89	readings, in terms of	U.S. Geological Survey technical report
4.1-03	90	relief, therefore, is	the book, *Natural Regions of the United States and Canada*
4.1-04	90	his brother, Ronald,	*Miami Herald* newspaper article
4.1-05	91	Las Vegas, NV	letter from the Nevada Gaming Control Board (letterhead)

Id	Page	Text	Source
4.1-06	91	`U.S. Geological Survey,`	U.S. Geological Survey technical report
4.1-07	91	`WASHINGTON, D.C.`	letter from the U.S. Mint (letterhead)
4.1-08	92	`4,500 3,500`	Battelle Pacific Northwest Laboratory technical report (table)
4.1-09	92	`4,300 residents`	*Kansas City Star* newspaper article
4.1-10	94	`forests;`	the book, *Natural Regions of the United States and Canada* (photo caption)
4.1-11	94	`layout;`	U.S. Department of Energy technical report
4.1-12	95	`MULTIPLIER.`	U.S. Geological Survey technical report
4.1-13	95	`consideration.`	U.S. Geological Survey technical report
4.1-14	96	`8.3.1.17.3`	U.S. Department of Energy technical report (table)
4.1-15	96	`In response,`	*San Diego Union-Tribune* newspaper article
4.1-16	96	`P.O. Box`	letter from the Chubb Life Insurance Company (letterhead)
4.1-17	97	`community,`	*National Geographic World* magazine article
4.1-18	97	`Berkeley, Calif.`	*Nation's Business* magazine article
4.1-19	98	`P.O. Box`	letter from AT&T (letterhead)
4.1-20	98	`busy, busy, busy.`	*Woman's World* magazine article
4.1-21	99	`Linda Blvd.,`	*Milwaukee Journal* newspaper article
4.1-22	99	`Planner.`	*Modern Maturity* magazine article
4.1-23	99	`Boulder, CO`	letter from *Consumer Reports* (letterhead)
4.1-24	100	`investigation.`	*New York Post* newspaper article
4.1-25	100	`and matching hat.`	*Ebony* magazine article (photo caption)
4.2-01	101	`"good" or "bad"`	*Good Housekeeping* magazine article
4.2-02	101	`"kriging."`	*Economic Geology* journal article
4.2-03	102	`"cold"`	Desert Research Institute technical report

Id	Page	Text	Source
4.2-04	102	subscript "o"	Los Alamos National Laboratory technical report
4.2-05	103	"birth" and "death"	University of California, Berkeley, technical report
4.2-06	103	"3-D"	U.S. Department of Energy technical report
4.2-07	104	"silicated"	Battelle Pacific Northwest Laboratory technical report
4.2-08	104	4-1/2" O.D.	U.S. Department of Energy technical report
4.2-09	105	"Power User"	letter from IMSI
4.2-10	105	"TO DELIMIT	U.S. Department of Energy presentation slide
4.2-11	106	`Help!'"	*National Geographic World* magazine article
4.2-12	106	for a dog,'" says	*Health* magazine article
4.3-01	107	*Initial	U.S. Department of Energy planning document (footnote)
4.3-02	107	R = G+H	International Nuclide Transport Code Intercomparison Study technical report
4.3-03	108	Account #	letter from Viking Office Products
4.3-04	108	proper-	U.S. Nuclear Regulatory Commission regulatory guide
4.3-05	109	& Conservation	U.S. Department of Energy technical report (table)
4.3-06	109	($6).	*Bon Appétit* magazine article
4.3-07	110	<2% of	Sandia National Laboratories technical report
4.3-08	110	% of	U.S. Environmental Protection Agency technical report (table)
4.3-09	111	50%	Sandia National Laboratories technical report (table)
4.3-10	111	71%	*Glamour* magazine article
5.1-01	116	Effects:	the book, *The Effects on Populations of Exposure to Low Levels of Ionizing Radiation* (page header)

Id	Page	Text	Source
5.1-02	116	Cliffhanger.	*Business Week* magazine article
5.1-03	117	albicaulis	Desert Research Institute technical report
5.1-04	117	Pinus longaeva	a book chapter, *Late Wisconsin Paleoecology of the American Southwest* (table)
5.1-05	118	Yedioth Ahronoth,	*Columbus Dispatch* newspaper article
5.1-06	118	Leaving	*San Diego Union-Tribune* newspaper article (headline)
5.1-07	119	Fenimore	*Life* magazine article
5.1-08	120	Customer Service	letter from Coca-Cola (letterhead)
5.1-09	120	0 mg chol.	*Sunset* magazine article
5.1-10	121	Office of the Dean	letter from the University of Texas at Austin (letterhead)
5.1-11	122	fear of financial	letter from Merrill Lynch
5.1-12	123	quarter of a million	*American Health* magazine article
5.1-13	123	I just got a job	letter from an individual
5.1-14	123	just like them	*National Geographic* magazine article
5.1-15	124	20305-1000	letter from the Defense Nuclear Agency (letterhead)
5.1-16	124	map of the	*Bulletin of the Geological Society of America* journal article
5.1-17	125	have to	*Mademoiselle* magazine article (title)
5.2-01	126	bigger	letter from the National Geographic Society
5.2-02	126	System	U.S. Department of Energy technical report
5.2-03	127	Operations	U.S. Department of Energy technical report
5.2-04	128	Congressional	U.S. Department of Energy planning document (table)
5.2-05	129	TOTAL	U.S. Department of Energy presentation slide
5.2-06	129	CONFIDENCE	Sandia National Laboratories presentation slide

Id	Page	Text	Source
5.2-07	130	*Definitions	U.S. Nuclear Regulatory Commission regulatory guide (footnote)
5.2-08	130	monitoring	U.S. Department of Energy public hearing transcript
5.3-01	131	Universal Studios	*Endless Vacation* magazine article (table)
5.3-02	131	Munson presented	*The American Legion* magazine article (photo caption)
5.3-03	132	National League of Cities,	*Boston Globe* newspaper article
5.3-04	132	The order	*Tampa Tribune* newspaper article
5.3-05	133	Fettuccine	*Seventeen* magazine article
5.3-06	133	until now	*Popular Science* magazine article
5.3-07	134	Meridian	*Barron's* newspaper article
5.3-08	134	easily understand it	*Working Woman* magazine article
5.4-01	135	DAILY	*Better Homes and Gardens* magazine article
5.4-02	136	New York, NY	*First for Women* magazine article (photo caption)
5.4-03	137	HOT WHEELS	*New York Daily News* article (heading)
5.4-04	137	UNIVERSITY OF NEVADA	letter from UNLV (letterhead)
5.4-05	138	MANAGING	*Nation's Business* magazine article (heading)
5.4-06	138	FUND	letter from the University of Illinois Foundation (letterhead)
5.4-07	139	FIDELITY	*Money* magazine article (heading)
5.4-08	140	If You	*Soap Opera Digest* magazine article (title)
5.4-09	141	RANCHO MIRAGE,	*Self* magazine article (heading)
5.4-10	141	AUGUST	*Star* newspaper article (heading)
5.4-11	142	74 FEBRUARY 1993	*Discover* magazine article (page footer)

Id	Page	Text	Source
5.4-12	143	IN BRIEF	*Atlanta Constitution* newspaper article (heading)
5.4-13	145	an	*Guideposts* magazine article (title)
5.5-01	146	Reporters	U.S. Department of Energy public hearing transcript (page footer)
5.5-02	147	BRIDGE PARKWAY	letter from the Benjamin/Cummings Publishing Company (letterhead)
5.5-03	147	MOWING	letter from an individual
5.5-04	147	DRINKING	*Health* magazine article (title)
5.5-05	148	What	*Modern Maturity* magazine article (title)
5.5-06	148	A Lot to Do	*Woman's Day* magazine article (heading)
5.5-07	149	SOUTH	*Country America* magazine article (heading)
5.5-08	150	Page A4, Column 4	*Wall Street Journal* newspaper article
5.5-09	150	T. 15 S., R. 70 E.	Nevada Bureau of Mines technical report
5.6-01	151	Africa	*Boston Globe* newspaper article (headline)
5.6-02	152	face	*New Orleans Times-Picayune* newspaper article (headline)
5.6-03	152	feds'	*Denver Post* newspaper article (headline)
5.6-04	152	ravaged	*Globe* newspaper article (headline)
5.6-05	153	SLAIN	*New York Post* newspaper article (headline)
5.6-06	153	RACE	*Hartford Courant* newspaper article (headline)
5.6-07	153	Cladding	Battelle Pacific Northwest Laboratory technical report (figure caption)
5.6-08	154	GOINGS	*Soap Opera Digest* magazine article (title)
5.6-09	154	TV TIMES	*Seattle Times* newspaper article (heading)
5.6-10	154	DIPLOMACY	*Vanity Fair* magazine article (title)
5.6-11	155	People	*Jet* magazine article (title)
5.6-12	155	Experiences	*Seattle Times* newspaper article (headline)

Id	Page	Text	Source
5.6-13	156	5	*Home Mechanix* magazine article (title)
5.6-14	156	Age	*New York Daily News* article (headline)
5.6-15	157	TEST	*Portland Oregonian* newspaper article (headline)
5.7-01	158	SettLingstones Mines	*Economic Geology* journal article (table)
5.7-02	159	semiquantitative sampLes)]	U.S. Geological Survey technical report (table)
5.7-03	159	Gatorade	*Consumer Reports* magazine article (footnote)
5.7-04	159	BLADE RUNNER	*Entertainment Weekly* magazine article (table)
5.7-05	160	Conshohocken, PA 19428	letter from Think Big! (letterhead)
5.7-06	160	EDUCATION STATISTICS, 1991;	*Reader's Digest* magazine article (footnote)
5.7-07	160	Workstation	letter from Andataco (letterhead)
5.7-08	161	VEGETABLE KABOBS	*Cooking Light* magazine article (photo caption)
5.7-09	161	ASSOCIATED PRESS	*Philadelphia Inquirer* newspaper article
5.7-10	161	REHABILITATION CENTER	letter from Saint Cloud Hospital (letterhead)
5.7-11	162	CORPORATION	letter from Access Long Distance (letterhead)
5.7-12	162	43.40 38.90	Sandia National Laboratories technical report (table)
5.7-13	163	0217-0031SC	U.S. Department of Energy planning document (page footer)
5.7-14	163	VC722A 12/14/93	letter from Davis Vision (page footer)
5.7-15	163	RAYBURN HOUSE	letter from a member of the U.S. House of Representatives (letterhead)

Index

About the Authors

STEPHEN V. RICE first encountered computers while pursuing a Bachelor's degree in mathematics at Western Michigan University in the late 1970s. His fascination with them led to his enrollment at the University of Illinois at Urbana-Champaign, where he earned a Master's degree in computer science. In the 1980s, he designed and implemented computer software in industry, with stints at IBM, Oracle, Synapse, and CACI, and with a two-year hiatus to teach computer science at San Juan College in New Mexico.

From 1991 to 1996, he served as the chief software engineer of the Information Science Research Institute (ISRI) at the University of Nevada, Las Vegas (UNLV), while earning a Ph.D. in computer science. He conducted the annual test of OCR accuracy and developed many of the performance measures used in the test.

His background and interests are wide ranging. Besides OCR, they include database systems, compilers, language design, user interfaces, graphics, simulation, computational geometry, sequence comparison, pattern recognition, and multimedia information retrieval.

He is now President of Comparisonics Corporation, where he invented the Comparisonics technology for content-based audio retrieval and display.

GEORGE NAGY was born of well-off but honest parents in Budapest. His interest in OCR was first kindled while learning to read in elementary school. After sporadic and ineffectual education in five countries, he was required to attend McGill University, where he divided his attention between engineering physics and contract bridge.

During his Ph.D. program at Cornell University, he participated in the construction of "Tobermory" under Frank Rosenblatt's direction. Tobermory was a four-layer perceptron that was almost able to understand continuous speech.

His research in pattern recognition at the T. J. Watson Research Center undoubtedly helped fuel IBM's explosive growth during the early 1960s. In 1972 he accepted an administrative appointment at the University of Nebraska where he also contributed imperceptibly to geographic information systems and computational geometry.

Since 1985 he has been professor of computer engineering at Rensselaer Polytechnic Institute. He continues to pursue his consuming interest in the shape and form of animate and inanimate objects: his current special interest is e/c dichotomies.

THOMAS A. NARTKER was trained in chemical engineering at the University of Dayton and the University of Tennessee in the late 1950s. He quickly learned that all of the important problems to be solved were both very large and very non-linear. In 1959, after a one-semester introduction to an IBM 650 at Texas A&M University, it became clear that digital computers were the solution to at least one of these problems. Since that time, he has continuously been involved with some aspect of computer science.

After completing requirements for the Ph.D. at Texas A&M in 1965, he accepted a position at New Mexico Tech as Computer Center Director and Chairman of a new Department of Computer Science. At Tech, he led the development of Bachelor's and Master's programs in computer science, and then a Ph.D. program in 1978.

From 1976 to 1981, he served as a Visiting Staff Member at Los Alamos National Labs working on programming languages for real-time data acquisition. In 1981 he joined the Shell Development Company in Houston to develop software for distributed process control.

He joined the Computer Science Department at UNLV in 1986, serving as Chairman for two years. In 1991 UNLV received funding to establish ISRI, an institute for applied and experimental research in Document Analysis and Information Retrieval, and he was appointed Director. One goal of ISRI research has been to identify the state of the art of technologies for recognizing characters from machine-printed documents. Another goal has been to understand the problems limiting progress in the field. This monograph is the culmination of six years of work in this area.

His interests range from document understanding to intelligent systems and from formal program derivation to programming languages and software engineering. Currently, he continues to direct work at ISRI and to teach courses in computer science.

GPSR Compliance
The European Union's (EU) General Product Safety Regulation (GPSR) is a set of rules that requires consumer products to be safe and our obligations to ensure this.

If you have any concerns about our products, you can contact us on

ProductSafety@springernature.com

In case Publisher is established outside the EU, the EU authorized representative is:

Springer Nature Customer Service Center GmbH
Europaplatz 3
69115 Heidelberg, Germany

www.ingramcontent.com/pod-product-compliance
Lightning Source LLC
Chambersburg PA
CBHW080715160426
43118CB00051B/466
* 9 7 8 0 7 9 2 3 8 4 9 2 2 *